CW00494437

FLAME TREE

Also by Kevin Hart

KEVIN HART

FLAME TREE

SELECTED POEMS

BLOODAXE BOOKS

Copyright © Kevin Hart 1978, 1981, 1984, 1981, 1995, 2002

ISBN: 1 85224 545 X

First published 2002 by
Bloodaxe Books Ltd,
Highgreen,
Tarset,
Northumberland NE48 1RP
and in Australia by Paperbark Press

www.bloodaxebooks.com
For further information about Bloodaxe titles
please visit our website or write to
the above address for a catalogue.

Bloodaxe Books Ltd acknowledges
the financial assistance of Northern Arts.

LEGAL NOTICE
All rights reserved. No part of this book may be
reproduced, stored in a retrieval system, or
transmitted in any form, or by any means, electronic,
mechanical, photocopying, recording or otherwise,
without prior written permission from Bloodaxe Books Ltd.

Requests to publish work from this book
must be sent to Bloodaxe Books Ltd.

Kevin Hart has asserted his right under
Section 77 of the Copyright, Designs and Patents Act 1988
to be identified as the author of this work.

Cover printing by J. Thomson Colour Printers Ltd, Glasgow.

Printed in Great Britain by
Cromwell Press Ltd, Trowbridge, Wiltshire.

to Rita

ACKNOWLEDGEMENTS

Poems in section I are taken from *The Departure* (University of Queensland Press) and *The Lines of the Hand* (Angus and Robertson), section II contains poems from *Your Shadow* (Angus and Robertson), section III includes most of *Peniel* (Golvan Arts), section IV comprises almost all of *Wicked Heat* (Paperbark Press), while section V consists of new poems.

'Dark Angel' alludes to a painting by Kristin Headlam of the same title. Previously uncollected poems have appeared in *Kenyon Review*, *Plastic*, *Poetry Review*, *Prism*, *slope*, *Stand* and *Southerly*. My thanks to all editors and publishers.

CONTENTS

I

1975-1979

The Lines of the Hand

It is foolish to look at the lines of my hand
And think they reveal my future,
That older man
Always turning round a corner just ahead.

I have followed him for years,
Always trying to glimpse his face, trying to catch
Any word he has to spare, trying
To judge him from his taste in clothes.

There are days I wake
And the room is full of him, mirrors stop me
And I see him: when I look outside
I see what he would see.

Once I saw an X-ray
Showing his hands clasped around my heart.
I tell myself I am the sun he is the moon
And when I stand quite still

My body casts two shadows,
Yet always I choose the wrong one to follow home
Where I find, as always,
Blank paper, a pen, and the lines of my face.

The Streets of Brisbane

When you arrive there
They will be waiting for you, and if it is raining
They will lead you
Under corrugated iron
Where you will taste the rusting air
Of Roma Street.

You will pass men in suits, sweating shadows,
Hurrying down streets named
After straightlaced English women
Who swam through the heat in fussy Victorian dresses
A world away from home.

Without warning
Evening will settle in all around you
And a street will lead you down to the river,
And you will see how lazy it is,
How fine, a long brown thigh, a woman
Reclining on her couch, just waiting for the cool of midnight,
The moon the only white on her body
As she lies there softly breathing, entirely naked.

Sin
(after César Vallejo)

If it rained tonight
I would go back a hundred years, and in that darkness
Believe my life was still to come.

Without a mother,
Without my lover's warm embrace,
Without this simple urge to sit and pray,

I would unstitch my fate, erase
Those lines I scored upon myself, untie
This cord that joins me to my death.

Yet even though I tell you this,
Although I tell myself *I have my time again!*
I cannot be free.

It is not the future
I fear, only what I have been, what I have done.

Four Ghazals

I

The forest does not need you to believe in it
But it will watch you sleeping, like an owl.

In a valley night comes suddenly, a slammed door;
Here, on the summit, the sun must cross an ocean.

There are always two forests: one speaks to birds,
The other to worms: a buried hand, alive.

Your foolish paths mean nothing to the forest.
What do you care for the parting in your hair?

Imagine all the people living Babel:
Each accent could be coloured a different green.

Nothing lasts longer than a night in the forest;
Any leaf can carry a night from years ago.

II

When the city of towers is destroyed
The city of broken glass begins its reign.

The maps of history use each colour;
But spin a map upon a pin: see, white.

The dead are queuing behind each one of us;
Tonight I felt one try to push in front.

What is it to be forgiven? To see again
The icon in a snowflake, light on old wood.

Certainly the dead will be our judges
But the unborn are in the Jury Room.

The steady thud as wood is chopped and falls;
My shadow crouches in the windy grass.

The leaves are darkening now, like old men's hands.
Soon winter will arrive with all his sticks.

Sunlight falls before the prisoner's feet;
He hears the scaffold hammered into place.

At evening my shadow measures the field;
I think of snow, the mandala in each flake.

The street rings with the coffin's final nail.
The grave is ready, we only await a death.

IV

Outside, a thick stillness: a wind grown old and white
Has crept into this valley to die.

I walk outside, feel fog curl down my throat,
And recall a Queen once drowned in milk.

All my shouts, my long sticks of torchlight, dissolve.
I hear the groping sheep, fog taught to sing.

Here and there I stumble on large, gray stones,
Odd places where the fog has calcified.

Moving towards me, walking into the real, a farmer
Clanking two buckets filled with fog, a soft offering.

All day I have walked the land of the dead,
But now I see a tree, each leaf with a spine of snow.

The Day Shift: Ford Works, London

At evening women in scarves return
To council houses with packages
Smelling of vinegar while their slim daughters

Fiddle with their hair
In shop windows that have become mirrors
As the street lights come on

About the Works,
The gray factual buildings beyond all change
Where, as the sky now deepens,

After all these years, with the smell of grease
I return and see
The day shift disperse across the yard,

Their hot breath clouding, and the boys
Forget their fight
And follow within their fathers' shadows.

My Death

Like the sun
I cannot bear to face it:
I say that it has nothing to do with me,

Exists outside of me, a silence
A darkness
When everything is done.

Yet even now
I feel it deep within me, closer
Than my breathing,

Moving within me, slow as my blood,
Measuring me
With all I care to do, a shadow

I follow
Or that follows me
And leads me to my centre not my edge.

Six Poems

Beside the paper
With today's black headline, an
Asterisk of snow.

*

Each day forces us
To totter on planks we hope
Will become bridges.

*

In the dead of night
I hear the clock talk, that white
Moustachioed face.

*

Sitting here alone:
Egg-timer like a woman,
The smell of onions.

*

All day and all night
The sea throwing a lace shawl
Over the fat rock.

*

Old, I try to see
The bright fish in the river
Through my reflection.

The Clocks of Brisbane

Yes, the Town Hall clock, big as the moon, shining over the Doric columns, the Square where a man walks, drawing in on a cigarette, watching the clock's hands draw together. The Vulture Street clock, with its grave Roman numerals, how it looks down on all the bars, the offices smelling of old typewriters. Or the clock at the Tennyson Power Station, hanging there amidst the factories, with cranes delicate as the husks of insects. That Post Office clock, its hands beginning to close, watching over Inala, now – when the moon is full and old – and when the moon is born again, new and unseen. The clock in that house, my father's house, there in the stillness of his living-room where pen, telephone and pipe are still and quiet except for a clock by a window endlessly counting the stars, its face white as the moon outside, and the moon rising on each fingernail of those inside, those wrestling in bed with the heat. They are all within the clock's hands, those in cheap hotels in the Valley, sprawling on mattresses smelling of beer, those out past Moggill where the black fields reek of mown paspalum, where mosquitoes whine away their lives in the thin wedges of minutes meted out by the clock's hands, those hands now nearly together, on the Town Hall, on the factories – Yes! the clocks are crying, Yes! Yes! – in the still living-room, in the man's bedroom, on his wrist, now, at midnight, as he joins his hands in prayer.

The Sea

1

The sea is very calm today. I guess that someone, for a bet, dropped a powder in the water and the whole sea set overnight.

Eventually, toward dawn, the whole crew gathers on deck. Someone says it looks like a field that's just been ploughed. Two sailors with hard-soled boots set off on the long walk to the nearest port for help, passing dolphins caught in mid-plunge with eyes still moving.

2

A small boat sets off from the dock toward the open sea. Soon it is a blur of smoke in the distance, and you return to the novel on your lap. But suddenly there's a *whoosh!* and you look up. The boat has finally cut the horizon and water is fountaining up, and children on the beach are jumping up and down shouting, 'A whale! A whale!'

The Stone's Prayer

Father, I praise you
For the wideness of this your earth, and for the sky
Arched forever over me,
For the sharp rain and the scraping wind
That have carved me from the mountain
And made me smooth as a child's face.

Accept my praise
For my colour, a starless night,
That my width is that between the first two stars of evening
Reflected in the water,
That my quartz flashes like lightning
And reflects the glory of your creation,

That you have seen fit
To place me near a stream and thus to contemplate
The passing of time;

For all that is around me I sing your praise,
For the fierce concentration of ants, their laws,
For all that they tell me about you.

Keep me, I pray, whole,
Unlike the terrible dust and pieces of bone
Cast about in the wind's great breath, unlike men
Who must suffer change,
Their endless footprints deep as graves;

Keep me in truth, in solitude,
Until the day when you will burst into my heavy soul
And I will shout your name.

Desire

It will open slowly, a night flower:
The moon's long fingers stroking your bare arms,
The courtyard with its jasmine breath
And all the warmth of blood.

This is the time
When bamboo knots in the night fields,
When girls uncurl from Roman frescoes,
Liquid as shadows, smelling of flowers and wine.

It would not take so long
If it did not rise from such pure depths:
A memory of what we must become,
The city in its lace of lights, the bay alive with sails.

It is within you, waiting,
The simple energy of evening, growing all day
To this: the moon burning in your hair,
Scent from an enclosed garden, the whites of your eyes.

For Jenny

It will come. All night I heard the ocean grieve
But now the first bird rises
Above the headland, slow as air in water.

And the summer, it will come
Regardless of what has been before, people lazily
Parting the heavy curtains of the heat.

Simply open yourself
And watch the change begin, a seagull burning
In morning's rush of light.

Our season will come
With the juice of orange and peach, and the dead
Will leave my mirror for good.

Open yourself and it will come,
As the ocean survives its long darkness, and the bird
Accepts all that is given.

Winter Portrait

Wakes, having dreamed
Pacific islands:
'Too cold to be Tahiti,'
She says, pulling herself

Up, blinking the room
Into place. The night
Cannot contain
Her dreams anymore,

They spill
Over: she dresses
Slowly, an exotic bird
Inspecting its feathers –

Eats raisins, mimes
A kiss, then hulas
Into the humming block
Of new, cold light

To bring back frozen milk.

The Yellow Christ
Gauguin

1

Here, with milkmaids at his feet,
Not far from a row of blue houses,
A man as yellow as the sun,

A man but not a man,
Although he carried a shadow like ours,
Although his face was lined like ours;

Here, in the centre of a field
Enclosed by hedges, already abandoned
By women and a man

Who must return
To a world that they can understand,
The Cross holds him a little above the world.

2

I know the distance between us
More than I know you, and you
Only as a darkness

That draws me like my own sleep;
Yet there can be no rest
With us forever apart, and I

Recoil into myself, I try to get by alone –
But see you always:
A face in the crowd, the curve between two hills,

And feel dead. And so
I try again, knowing
No reason why you should come half-way

But you do,
Here, in Brittany, in a simple field,
The sky heavy with rain, the apple trees in blossom.

The Twenty-First Century

When we arrive there
With our guns, our machinery, our heavy books,
There will be so much to say,

And we will sit down
Over cigars and cognac and tell our stories
Of minor battles, mirages, times when it seemed
That no one would survive.

And we will talk only about ourselves,
Forgetting our fathers
And all they did, their belief that the future
Was only as good
As their plans for it,
And that we grew to be the same.

Then we can finish our stories in peace,
When the wars
Are no longer ours to fight,

When we no longer have the clenched fists
Of our youth, and our children have inherited
The terrible certainty
That we have ruined all we have been given,

And our hands will be empty,
We will have nothing to give, only our stories
Of how everything we should have held before us
Like a candle
Was lost, forgotten, as we made our way
Across the fields of sadness, walking towards the horizon.

The Horizon

Whenever you take a step
I am with you leading you meeting your eyes.
I am here at dawn watching
The old priest hurrying to Mass
Ready to greet him with my gift of blood.

How easily I shed the clothing
You try to give me,
You who cannot bear to see me as I truly am
Your trees mountains buildings I have no time for them.

I was here
Before the stone received its hardness,
This entire world could not be conceived
Before the thought of me.

You comfort yourselves:
You say I am only a line never reached
That I do not exist as you do
But none of this is true:
You see only the top line of my head
Beneath that I have the world
With all its fields sun moonlight and rain.

You who hate departures,
You who forever try to shut me out
Listen to me:
Whenever you think of death,
Whenever you enter the room of someone gone from you,
I will be peering through the window.
I will catch you
Even though my net has just one string.
You have no need for mirrors
Who lie to you until it is too late,
Look at me and see the only truth
Your past what you are now
All your future sorrows and your only blessing.

Silence

There is the silence of hills
That lodges tightly inside each hill,
The silence of the sky
Rounded forever above the earth,
The silence of the poppy as it dreams of red,
The silence of the stone
And of the string once the hand has withdrawn,
The silence between words
That cannot bear them to burn alone,
That gives of itself until exhausted, a breeze in the flame.

To Our Lady

Mother of all that is good,
Of the light that is always touching this world
Blessing all things,
The efficient system of each leaf,
The dark impasses of the lines of my hand,

You tell us
Of the stone's astonishment
At the sudden warmth of a first beam of light,

Of the horizons of dust
That cry to the clouds, *Give us your fullness*
And let us live,

You take from us
The mounds of darkness we bury inside of us
And make from them a night of stars
Where we can see your Son:

Our Lady,
Withheld from death,
Mother of all things that must die,
Speak for us:
Do what we cannot do ourselves,
Help us to hold in our hands the bird in flight,
To pull from our feet our heavy shadows, to walk your way.

The Street

A long dark street in the east end of London. No one about and only one window alight, a small screen showing a film concerning the travesties of war. This section features a girl, about twenty, in her bedroom removing make-up before a mirror, pausing now and then to look at a photograph of a man in uniform who smiles back from two years before. The film is poorly made and rather sentimental, so I walk on – and realise that the rows of houses are the front lines of two armies deadlocked in battle, that they have been frozen here for years, and I am perilously picking my way through no man's land. In their grey faces I see the frenzies once fought over in the Somme, and see now that the girl does not exist. She is only a memory coming to light in one of the soldier's minds.

I am of course walking through a vast exhibit in a museum, made larger than life so that its point will not be missed by even the most cursory visitor. The girl is, as I suspected, on film, a clever mechanical device springing to life when anyone passes. At the end of the street I see the full moon which doubles as a clock for the entire museum. It tells me that it is much later than I had thought, that I have stayed too long, that the museum is closed and I am locked in for the night. Nothing to do now but wait until morning, as all these dead have been waiting for years.

Pozières

The moon shines over the field,
It looks at itself from the bottom of the Somme;
It enters the houses of Pozières
And spills across the tables, hard as salt.

Over the church with its burning candles,
Over the white-haired man still drinking,
The moon looks down.
                        This face is deepest white,
This face remembers nothing. And the people sleep,
And the moon enters their dreams:
A clock that says it is all over now,
A plate that says eat all you wish.

And at the bottom of the old man's glass
The moon sparkles like a coin, but his face remains dark
Like the other face of the moon.

Prague, 1968

1

As if the entire population but you
Slipped off the globe at night: so you wake
To find the house empty, the kind of silence
That hunts round abandoned aerodromes,
And quicken outside, hoping to find someone
But feel a carbine thrust in your back,
A burst of rapid consonants from behind...
It must have happened while you dreamed. He leads
You off, across the city, past mounds of things
Still burning, tanks blundering down streets
Much faster than you'd think, until the distant
Thunder of orders, tanks, guns, contracts
To a crowded Square where soldiers raise their flag,
Divide those captured into groups, open trucks,
And collect your first row, then your second...

2

As if you somehow slipped off the globe
During the night: you wake a little early
In a foreign room, your clothes are here
And next door someone is eating noisily.
Terrible things have happened. Outside,
Men are walking to work, sullen as pewter,
You hope no one thinks you different
And quicken past the soliders at the corner
Fingering their guns that seem so big,
Speaking grudgingly, a winter gutteral.
It is too cold for a dream: your breath
Hangs like the clouding smoke from the nearby tank
That points you, with the rest, to the Square.
What is happening? The old man beside you
Is trembling like the edge of a flag.

3

As if you had somehow stepped into a dream
Walking one night through Wenceslas Square,
You see a distant flagpole begin to tilt
Then sweep the sky, some soldiers march past
A balding man who turns into a shadow
And presses against a wall. Now home,
You remember waking early, and seeing
The sky full of mushrooms floating down,
Becoming men with guns once they touch the ground.
After the first week it was not strange,
Not hearing the paper's dull thud on the porch,
Seeing the tank swivelling its head
While shopping in the Square, the children off school
Playing soldiers in the house all day
And the city bristling with spires and searchlights.

The Family

(after Jacques Prévert)

The mother, she knits,
The son fights in the war, he does his bit,
And mother finds that it all fits.
And father, what does he do?
He works at his office, he sits –
His wife, she knits,
And his son, he does his bit
While father goes to the office and sits
And finds the whole thing all fits.
And the son, the son,
What does he think can be done?
He thinks of nothing, of not being hit;
His mother she knits, his father he sits,
And he, he does his bit.
And when the war is done,
He will sit beside his father, the son.
But war continues, mother continues to knit
And father continues to sit.
The son is hit – he does not continue –
So father and mother
They go to the graveyard to visit
And somehow find that it all fits.
And life takes breath,
Life with its knitting and sitting,
Its sitting and knitting and doing one's bit,
The perpetual knitting of life and death.

The Old

You cannot forget the old.
They become part of you.
They take you for themselves.

I have watched them in the city.
They stack themselves up
Against the walls like chairs.

They always seem to be waiting
For something to happen.
It never does.

Or if it does I'm never there.
I do not trust them.
They aren't satisfied with death.

They keep on coming back.
Someone old will be inside your flesh
Not long from now,

Taking you over completely
Going about your business
Sleeping with your wife.

I know the one who wants me.
Sometimes I think I know his thoughts.
He will know me very well,

But still we won't get on.
He will walk for miles
Just thinking of me.

It will be very much like love.
He will leaf through old books
Where I have written silly things.

He will search out photograph albums
And stare at pictures of me,
Adjusting old white corners

Smelling the gum.

A History of the Future

There will be cities and mountains
As there are now,

And steeled armies
Marching through abandoned Squares
As they have always done.

There will be fields to plough,
The wind will shake bright trees, acorns
Will fall,

And plates will still crack
For no apparent reason.

And that is all we can truly know.

The future is over the horizon, we cannot hear
A word its people say,

And even if they shout to us
To make us cease
Bombing their lands, destroying their cities,

A shout from there would sound like an acorn
Dropped on cement,

Or a plate on the shelf
Beginning to crack.

Three Prayers

Master of energy and silence
    Embracer of contradictions
Who withdraws behind death
    Like horizons we never touch
Who can be One and Many
    Like light refracting through glass,

Stepping in and out of logic
    Like a child unsure of the sea
In and out of time
    Like an old man dozing, waking,
In and out of history
    Like a needle through cloth,

Who we chase and bother with theories
    Who hides in equations and wind
Who is constant as the speed of light
    Who stretches over the Empty Place
Who hangs the Earth upon Nothing
    Who strikes like lightning.

*

Master of light, my God,
Before whom stars tremble
And fall into themselves,

Who glows within each thing
Beyond reach of language
And deeper than silence,

Who passes through the dark
That draws us towards death
And makes it one with you,

Whose light is everywhere
Wherein I stand and see
My shadow disappear.

*

You do not speak to me of death.
You do not pester me, like some.

Far too busy with the universe,
Sometimes not busy enough,

Searching out our softer parts,
Trying to squeeze yourself in:

Showing off your famous night sky
Like a child with a new drawing,

Forever posing impossible problems
We try to solve like crosswords:

So when I wake and see the ceiling
Mottled like an old man's skin

I think of you,
When I imagine the grinning dead

I think of you,
And also when, at night,

I sometimes wake to find
A hand slowly stroking my thigh.

Praying for the Dead

And in the church, silence.
The beautiful dead
Assemble: they creep

From chalices, the choir,
Gold candlesticks,
And hang above the pews

Like clouding breath.
Conjured by hymn and ritual
They glow, human,

Exhausted by the earth.
They waver like small hot flames
Impatient with the little we have to say.

For them, everything is lucid,
Now finally released
From the tangle of their lives

And each doubt cancelled.
They rise and dissolve like incense –
The night sky's waning lights

Are beckoning them home.
They will be taken for shadows.
They will be blamed for everything.

Some nights they will be
Smoke above the river,
Some nights

The cold worlds of the icons.
Theirs is the silence
At the end of all our talk,

Their answer
To all our questions, all our hopes,
Wordless as the priest

Eating the bread and wine,
Or the simple crosses
Pointing downwards.

II

1980-1983

If an object is opaque and dark, it makes a dark shadow; if it is transparent and delicate, its shadow is transparent and delicate. Thus the shadow of a dark object amounts to another darkness in the measure of the darkness of the object, and the shadow of something bright amounts to something else that is bright according to the brightness of the object.

ST JOHN OF THE CROSS

The Ten Thousand Things

The lemon trees fatted with sunlight,
The terraces laced with jasmine,
The whisper of her white dress –

These ten thousand things of the world
That cling like honey.

But see the wind,
How it can find no home
Among the trees, how the stones
Care nothing for the earth, their roots
Curled up within themselves.

Calm beyond reason,
They ask us to accept the solitude
Of homeless things, to forego
The sunlight growing wild upon the water,
That we might know
The endless dark inside a stone.

They will teach you
To look with care upon this world
That cares for nothing,
To forget
The girls dawdling in the orchard,
The locked skeletons of fighting reindeer,

And you will see
At evening, dark roots
Clutching the earth, drawing new life
From the river where you have found
The true man's face, once hidden by your own.

Your Shadow

Fed by its eye, the falcon
Swims with the flooding wind, watching
Its shadow writhe
Like something left half-dead.

Open your hand
And see the darkness nursed there, see how
Your shadow blossoms,
Your body's very own black flower.

It is a gift, a birth right, your baby shawl
Now growing into a shroud;
You are an eye, intent upon this world,
It is your pupil, shining.

Come closer, it is a trap-door
Into the secret earth, and one day soon
You will go there
To meet the child you were, covered with dirt.

It will not hurt you, it simply shows
That you are not alone,
That what you fear is part of you,
That you are both the killer and the kill.

This Day

The clock above stalled traffic, white as bread;
Women, serving time, spilling out from factories;
My grandfather breathing in sawdust like pepper;

Greek women in black, like olives; men in bars
Watching their drinks begin to watch them back:
This day, a compass pointing in all directions.

Newspapers with headlines like ink-blot tests;
A red telephone, ringing, as if boiling over:
This day, a flame burning inside each one of us.

Mosquitoes humming like a tuning-fork just struck;
The moon, the sun's disguise; girls dressed to kill,
And thoughts, like sharpened knives, behind the eye.

This day, sometimes a ship, sometimes an ocean:
That man who wears his dead wife's wedding ring;
The clock above the darkened city, like a host.

Keys turned in locks; grease wiped from chins;
The strange rituals of those who believe in death.
This day, done with, like a nail hit once and bent.

Jerusalem

This is where the deserts end.
This is the city where the dead still live.
Here, at evening,
The sun and moon are both still full,
And when you arrive
The road can take you nowhere else.
Enter this inn
And see its empty table, its dead fire,
This window where
Those distant mountains stare into the past.

Remember
That woman with a broken jar,
That young man
Feeding swine in the sad desert twilight.

They say that silence leads us here,
That we are led
As if by hand, wind running fingers through the dust;
Inside, the silence
Will take you by the hand.
Here you bow to enter doors;
Here, a man once came
As one of us
To speak of all that we are not.

Now feel this stillness
Where two opposing forces clasp: this is the room
Where bread is broken
To make us whole, the inn of our desire.

Midwinter Summer

Summer before the thought of summer
And I see you bend
To the magnolia's stark green
To coax the blossom out,
As if the season could be made to stay.

The day feels wrong
As if two days had come disguised as one,
Or God had reconsidered overnight
And made another world
Without a winter, where nothing dies.

My room is quiet and heavy, and last night I found
My grandfather's watch
Stuck to a past midday or midnight.
When I freed its hands
I heard the pounding of my pulse.

You sit outside today, dressed in white
Like the magnolia in summer
And like my grandfather's watch;
And as though this other world would last, my love,
I go to be with you.

The Storm

1

My garden falls quiet, falls in the darkest of moods,
Not wanting me around this afternoon.

But as I turn to go
A thrill runs up the leaves' spines
And dirt smells sweet.

And then
The storm strikes:

With claws that slash my window.

2

Ah, let it have that washing on the line

And let it take the shed roof for a trampoline –
What do I care,
So long as I hear water whooping through the drains...

Let it frisk the tree for sparrows and their eggs

And let it pry into each crack in those loose tiles
And tell me that houses fall:

I need to learn that nothing lasts.
                                    Lord knows,
I have to learn it fresh each year.

3

But it is good to know, also,
That the soul is hail thrashing a stone wall
                    and not always a lake in moonlight,
And who in the world would show me that?

So let the storm veer out to sea:

Already it has given
                    more than I wanted of today,
Something I cannot put down

Now or ever.

Your Shadow

It is the thing
Beside you when you wake, a cold sheet
As delicate as your skin.

It is the lie
Hunched within each word you say,
The stain you cannot clean;

The reserve of evening
That will sustain you through the day,
The blueprint

For the monster in your head,
The sideshow mirror
Whose black humour is all too true.

You are a window
And everyone can see inside; your shadow
Means protection, a curtain

Whose darkness discloses
You live in a tight corner, out of the light,
While on this earth.

You are, as always,
Standing on the brink of something new,
And your shadow

Waits behind, paring its nails,
And it will follow you
Across the earth, until it brings you home.

Midsummer

These are the richest weeks
When light slows to heat, when all that grows
Fattens with the sweetest juices:
And this cloudless sky
So heavy, as though we walked through cloud.

Green summer has come
And you are dressed in white.
Simply to be here now, in the heat's stunned silence,
With all of time ahead, to think to it
As something given, a garden.

Forget the listless nights,
The darkness that will not accept our roots,
The wasps among hot poppies,
The soldiers marching past the orchard.
Our day is here, today,

And even tomorrow has begun
Though far away from us, in towns still cold,
In grasping hands,
In rooms where spiders dream of lace.
It will be all that was promised,

Tomorrow, the new land,
As though I had never touched you before:
Another day, as rich as this,
A garden in blossom, a river's hush, the promise
Renewed through change: this world.

Flemington Racecourse

The racehorses assemble at the starting barrier
In all the finery of a medieval pageant, the jockeys
In silks like figures from a Tarot pack,

The bookies in leather and tweed, beside their boards,
Each hoping that the future has been controlled;
And everyone, except the dissembling birds, is still –

Concentrating on a frisky tail, a flashing red light.
They go, against the clock, leaving the shouting crowd
In noisy elegance, with jockies stretching necks

And fathers jumping up onto their seats.
The electronic timer divides time into its hairs
As the horses break ground, continually printing

The earth with emblems of good fortune, all leaning
Toward the fence, bunched up and fighting, until
Two suddenly break free from the pack, and only the timer

Is beating them, each number something impulsive
And longed-for, like life continuing after death.
Thousands have come to watch, forgetting cars, yet

At the turn nothing can be seen: there is only
The sound of a storm approaching, streamlining
On the straight into the particulars of faces

Straining to be the first to get the future over with.
Only the timer is heartless now, and the manic voice
Of the commentator, like a loud typewriter, crams

Each new second with more words than ever before.
Our eyes will tell us so much more, how one horse
Now leaves the others easily, like a fresh runner

Just handed a baton, how it pushes through the air
As though the final run were straight downhill.
The future has fooled the past, then joined its ranks –

It's autumn with paper leaves, and even the brilliant,
Evil mind of the timer stops as the horses slow down,
Their ordeal over now, and all of time before them.

For Marion, My Sister

In London, where the hospital
No longer rises above the rising skyline,
I almost find you
In faces older than the houses.
Listen to me,
Try to make out my words
Though death has pushed in front of language;
Try to imagine
This world behind the nails and instruments.
I have tried to go back
Further than I can, thumbing through the album
To find the page before the cover,
And I am tired of it.

I say your name
Though it reminds me of nothing, like water.
Your silence makes me think
Of clutching ice, watching
Its needles slowly dissolving in my hand.

I tell myself
I have been you in the mirror
Before I see myself, a boy-girl face
That weds us before I think.
This will not do,
My face is different
And I must have it whole. See here my hands
Balancing a future
Withheld from you, a lake becoming a river.

I have not stolen it, my sister,
And cannot give it back.
I do not know
Why you were chosen
And I was not, I cannot understand
What brings you,
Thirty years too late,
Back from the other world: only

Tonight I feel you
As our mother once felt you,
Trapped in a cage deep within me,
Beating steadily
With articulate, insistent fists.

The Hammer

Grasping the handle he is suddenly one with the hammer;
He feels its worn wood, polished with sweat, and closes
Deeply around it as though hands were made for hammers

And men to be controlled by hammers: it makes him stand
Feet slightly apart, breathing evenly, concentrating
On nothing but a three-inch nail. Drained now of both

Past and future, existing only in this dense block
Of sunlight where nothing must be wasted, not even
The untutored beatings of the heart, he slowly raises

One arm backwards not lifting an eye and trusting his aim
As without a word a soprano reaches for her top note.
This is the sanctus, the pause for preparation, for

Pushing the mind's energies tightly into muscle;
This is the archer's erasure of himself from his tense
Matrix of forces, the moment of conditioned release

When the mind delights in its freedom to step outside
And adore the body, a perfected instrument of will.
And so the instant comes, intense and blurred, the head

Strikes the nail through the knotted grain, jumping
Back as though appalled by such precise violence, and
For a moment containing the man's mind, pure energy.

The Beast

Whatever it is you've given me
It's something I cannot control, some wild thing
Pawing inside me, an animal
Swung by the tail and thrown inside a cage.

All day I feel its claws,
Its burning moods; it's broken all I own
And makes me live in a country
Lit only by storms,
                or sits up late with me, in a room
Pierced by a brazen music.

A wolf and lamb in one, the taste
Of honey and gall! I've done nothing
Yet this thing hunts me from within
And my body aches
As if rubbed with crushed glass.

It has no grace, no manners;
            I've tried to reason but it backs off
Into a corner, snarling. And yet

It's made me know the strageness
Of the seed when the tree inside begins to kick,
The river's longing
When it feels the ocean's pull.

I've tried to feed it
But it grows daily, and when I starve it
I feel it scratching my heart.

You've given me this animal you've bred;
Tell me, can it be tamed?
I cannot live with it or bear to let it go;
Already I love it, even its claws.

North

The dead heat of evening, the thoughts of the day –
Those flowers' loose, thin, snake-like tongues; the lake
Reflecting sunlight like an insect's eye;

And squeezed between two mountains, that waterfall –
A river that tries to stand and walk away.
All day spent roaming through a photograph,

The sun intent on filming us in close-up.
The jungle breathes this heat, even asleep
When no one else can sleep, the fine mosquitoes

That score their names upon our peeling skin.
Here we forget the spirit, the essence of light,
And think only of our bodies' weight;

The birds' red-yellow screech; the crickets' pulse;
Flies in the web, their wings like drops of oil;
The tap in the kitchen tapping out the time;

The tinkling of ice in a glass, a piano's high notes.
Just lying here together, breathing the same air
And thinking of sleep. Too hot for making love.

Flies

(after Antonio Machado)

I could never get rid of you
No matter what the room or street:
At meals, kissing my first girl, walking by the river,
You joined me
And now you bring it back to me.

I don't know what minute books you read
Upon my ceiling –
The prayers of fallen angels, perhaps –
You sing the song
The radio plays between its channels.

On summer afternoons
When the sun has halved the day's allowance of air,
You dart around
Like tadpoles in the coolest water
And make me feel as heavy as my bed.

I've watched your dated soft-shoe act
On blackboards, nuns, and men with picks;
And when, inflamed with Marx,
I gave up God,
You sang of the equality of flies.

But I know
That you have rested on my oldest toys,
Upon my Latin grammar,
My love letters, and my grandfather's dying face.
I know you live off filth, I know

You never work like bees
And certainly never shine like butterflies;
And yet, old friends,
This morning as I hear you buzz
You bring my past all back to me, like honey and light.

The Will to Change

This stone brimming with darkness, this weed
Taking its first breath,
This body intent upon the pure moment,

Will change: they are leaning into the future
And the future
Is bending like a river bank.

It is the guts of things, that petrol works
Outside the city limits
At night, displaying flags of flame,

A bonsai metropolis
Flowing with power, a constellation fallen
Into this world of change.

Or the city centre
With cars like bees all clinging to the comb,
Its shop windows

A continuous film of desires, and
The shop girls
With their faces sharpened by make-up.

The music in your room
Will change the room into itself, it will
Undress the objects around you

And you will feel
The sudden nakedness of pouring water.
Come, be quickened

Like a river approaching the rapids,
You must see
You are moving towards yourself, the one

Who will give up this world
As the afternoon blossoms from the cool morning,
As the flame reaches from the wood.

Sunlight in a Room

The silence attending words,
The body firm as a plum
And the spirit now weightless
And willing as a needle,

And gathering around me
This summer morning, sunlight
Basking on the wooden floor
With an animal pleasure:

This first, thoughtless joy, the taste
Of chill water, as the sun
Places bread upon a sill,
A hand upon my lover.

Your Shadow

Not the one in mirrors,
Not the one shut up in photographs,
Not the one who feels her hand at night,
Not the one who trusts in words:

The one without a face,
Who sways with your each movement, the snake-charmer;
Who keeps his ear to the ground,
Who puts on circus stilts when evening comes.

This is the one
The sun has given you for company;
A fallen guardian angel,
A butterfly stuck to its chrysalis.

How quiet he is, your friend,
And how attentive to your each need –
As the ocean caresses the shore,
As the bee trembles beside a blossom;

He will not let you die, so you
Must trust in him more than your heart:
One day you will become
That other man, the silent one, the one in black.

The Members of the Orchestra

Walk onto the dark stage dressed for a funeral
Or a wedding and we, the anxious ones, quieten
And wait to discover which it will be tonight:

They sit or stand before thin books written
In a foreign script, more alien than Chinese,
But its secret contents will be revealed now

As at the reading of a dead relation's will,
For the last member has entered, slightly late
As befits his honour, like a famous lecturer

With a new theory and a pointer to make it clear.
Alas, he too cannot talk except in the language
Of the deaf and dumb, but as he waves his hands

The members of the orchestra commence their act
Of complicated ventriloquism, each making
His instrument speak our long-forgotten native tongue.

Now one violin reaches above the rest, rehearsing
The articulate sorrow of things in this world
Where we have suddenly woken to find a music

As curious as the relation between an object
And its name. We are taken by the hand and led
Through the old darkness that separates us

From things in themselves, through the soft fold
Of evening that keeps two days apart. And now
Each instrument tells its story in details

That become the whole, an entire forest contained
Within a leaf: the orchestra is quickly building
A city of living air about us where we can live

And know ourselves at last, for we have given up
Our selves, as at our wedding or our funeral,
To take on something new, something that was always there.

Mountains

They will come for you,
The colour of stormclouds, the weight of oceans.

They will cross deserts, cities,
And lean upon you through a window.

Do not ask them when,
Their words would be too hard to bear;

But if you walk upon a mountain
Listen for a voice in the throats of birds.

You cannot distract them,
Their faces gaze away from you, lost

In the mindlessness of space.
But watch them closely,

They will tell you more than mirrors:
See how the fields slope away from them,

How at evening they become the evening
And settle around your shoulders.

The South Pole

This is the place one reaches
When everything is finished, this cold world
Beneath the world
Where water finds its grudging home
In a grasp of needles.

Walking here
I have become fine glass
The slightest noise will shatter;
These open plains
A pause between the clock's

Sullen, empty strokes;
They last forever like the final moment
Before the advent of sleep,
Like the horizon
As it sweeps across the world, a wind

Scraping all it finds
Down to the stretching, rotted root.
It is a form of purity,
The knife's flash, a final reduction
To the zero waiting

At the equation's end;
A lightness that registers
Long after the pain has gone, after
One no longer sees
The clock's hands refusing to hold the world,

But only the white
From which there can be no escape
Once you are strapped into the pack,
Once the weight
Is commonplace, no longer regretted or desired.

The Real World

Rays of sunlight quietly fishing from tall trees;
A wrestler, smoking, his fingers fat as toes;
Old men in bars, with arms that end in glass;
A haloed moon tonight, a hole within a hole.

Steel factories like German concentration camps;
The orchestra, tuning, mixing its new palette;
Myers deserted at night, a museum from the future;
And tying shoelaces, a hole that's through a hole.

Rain pecking at the window-pane; a dripping star
That took a thousand years to find this lake;
A discotheque bulging with mirrors and music;
A black hole, a hole in space, that hole.

That blade of sunlight shaving Africa;
Pipe smoke curling slowly upwards, a cobra's ghost;
The child's black pupil with its coffin's shine.
And a hole within a hole that's through a hole.

Old Man Smoking a Pipe

Folding back into his chair
He takes something the doctor might have left,
An instrument
That brings back all his past.

Smoke rises:
A girl's warm breath in winter,
A rearing horse,
That fragrant loaf
Still feeding him after fifty years.

Outside,
The sun sits on the church,
A brass bell, calling
The sleeping to swim up through deep pools;

And on the table
A small knife, matches, the forgettable things
That compose a life.

The tobacco
As brown as a young soldier's hair
Preserved
In a glass jar a family memento;
But once alight

It turns gray as this man's hair
As the minutes pass and a life is considered
And finally understood.

Your Shadow

At daylight
It is already obsessed,
Wearing black as if expecting your funeral
And trying to be a grave.

All morning the sun tries to distract,
Displaying mountains, offering flowers,
Then, furious,
Burns it within an inch of life
At noon, when it crawls in under your feet.

But watch: it returns
Vast, superior, freshened by failure and rest,
And noses ahead of you like a dog
Or lags behind,
Sprawling on the pavement peering up dresses.

It sees you as fat, dwarfish, beneath contempt;
And, dreaming of victory,
Stretches its long tentacles to others, pulling
Until your last strength goes.

Your only hope:
Turn on a light, quickly,
Then, a fisherman, you can hold a slithering catch
Like this strange thing
Still clambering to get out my window –
Defeated,
Though not for long.

To the Spirit

I find you as I remember the sun whenever I strike
A match, and find myself somewhere on the outskirts
Of the milky way, but close to you; like the road

Stationed outside my door that set out so long ago
From Babylon, you find me fiddling with my watch, or
You come so suddenly, as something long forgotten,

Taking me over completely, a grain of salt in water.
I am like the sea trying to straighten myself out
On a beach while ships are sinking elsewhere, yet

You find me as the ocean receives a stream widening
Beyond itself, becoming the beaten foam, a rain
That falls only upon the sea, a plunging undertow.

The star's last breath of light still crosses space
And so I find you, both then and now; I am within you
Always, as within the whole of language; always, as

The universe forever forms itself: unfolding
With each new gesture of the blossoming tree, the wind
That shakes its fruit, the man who tastes its flesh.

Come Back

Come back to me.
The road is waiting quietly outside your door,
The wind is blowing the leaves this way.
It is late afternoon,
The best time for making love; half the world
Is sleeping now: no longer sad
The violins fit
Into their velvet cases, and lovers there
Must do without their eyes.
Come back. I want to tell you how
All of the things I only half-believed before
Are true, I want to find
That part of you I never touched
And make it blossom,
I want the clock to count the hours as seconds
Until your sorrow is forgotten.

Come back.
Don't watch the sunlight lazing on the street,
Don't wait for fruit to grow without a rind.
You know the way,
The heat that's in the flesh by afternoon,
The taste of salt,
The face that fits into your eyes.
I want to know, again,
What it's like to breathe your words;
I want to know, once more,
How it feels
To be peeled and eaten whole, time after time.

Four Poems

Going through old clothes
I find a single blonde hair –
All I have of her.

*

Just to be with her
I'd cut off both nose and ears
Though not lips or eyes.

*

That entire summer
We made love, and now she's gone
I still cannot sleep.

*

Her tongue in your mouth,
Her hand just where it should be –
But her mind with him.

The House

I left that city on a summer evening, the streets felt stale with the heat of many summers. The office blocks with their cool lights were like old, cumbersome computers still solving the problems of the past. My car was more efficient, and soon the road was liquid and curving, yet easily straightened by my wheel. Soon I was passing through the slow hours when the landscape is barely watched and almost ceases to exist, when the soul is joined to the body by a single thread; and in the distance I could make out the city of my birth. My father had died, suddenly, and there was much to be done.

The industrial suburbs were deserted, except for a man lighting a cigarette in the heavy shadows of a car factory. Once in the city I parked, glad to move about, and idled past bars where men sat hunched over drinks like beakless birds. I decided to walk the four miles to the house, breathing in the dark air, watching my image rise and fall in windows of small tobacconists and barbers. Finally, at the end of a street, there stood that tree I had once tried to climb, leafless now, and from each branch there hung faces of the family, men with moustaches and pipes, women with faces fine as spiderwebs.

I came upon the house from behind, and saw it as the dead must see their lives, as something odd and ungainly to have won such love. Tired now, I found my former room, crammed with old furniture and dustmotes gliding through the moonlight. Lying down I began to slip away from the world, becoming the size of myself in a photograph, myself reflected in an eye. Like father, I could see my life from the other side – unfinished, all hidden errors exposed – like a needle pushed through embroidered cloth.

The End of Summer

The holiday game is almost over,
This is the last move of summer.
The garden fans itself asleep,
A peacock hiding behind its tail.

Tired of standing on the sidelines
The sun assumes the centre stage.
A clock tries, for a moment,
To hold the day with just one hand.

And the earth I once trusted
Has stolen my shadow, a trial run
Before it takes my body at death.
The sun has tipped the scales.

It is so quiet now, I hear
A warm breeze preening the tree.
The clouds pass over quickly
As if required elsewhere soon.

The afternoon grows stale
As the clock's spring unwinds.
The forces of darkness return;
My own shadow holds me in check.

Your Shadow's Songs

sit tibi copia nostri

The angel of death is older now
And finds the pleasures of the flesh

Too tiring, closing dead men's eyes
A job he'd rather do without.

Almost human, he loves this world –
The bitter ocean's opal fish,

The tall glass buildings filled with light –
But sees the future, jammed in reverse,

Out of control; the cheating senses
Like a hand about each throat;

The field of blood within the heart.
Grown wiser now, he knows God's mind,

Why in this best of possible worlds
He has no day of rest: he sees

More clearly than Gabriel the mind
That twists within the human skull.

Adoring the God behind God's face
Each day he comes to draw his line

Between the language of the blessed
And this, the language of the lost.

Midnight and noon, the fear of death –
You hate the man who wears your face.

The mind takes root in mounds of dirt
And sunlight cuts the world in half

But still your shadow grows, and sin
Has carved its name upon your flesh.

A child is born and wrapped in lace,
A knife is placed upon its tongue;

You close both eyes and only find
A darker shadow cast inside.

You want to hold God in your hand,
To peel the river from its banks:

You try to paint your shadow white,
Your heart always too young to help.

The door is locked, the windows barred;
Upon your knees you beg the clock

To scrape your shadow from the floor
And hide it in your father's grave.

Your shadow simply points ahead
And you will never lose the way.

My brother, when you fed on blood
Our mother smiled to feel each kick,

You slid into a world of light
And found me in the doctor's arms;

I saw the world that God had made
Was signed beneath with death's thick cross,

And watched you grow a grave's full length
Before you looked out with my eyes.

I know you all too well, this head
That holds its thoughts like mercury,

This soul composed of ice and steam,
So trust me when I say the dead

Are busy at their feast of earth,
The clock is locked into first gear;

Our God has cast us in this world
Not into hell: one flesh, two minds,

Identified in the one light,
And swept together in the same wind

Till death when all of life contracts
About you, like your shadow at noon.

Whose world is this? I walk with you
And try to think of earth as home;

I sleep with you, your bony arms
Holding me closer than your soul,

So that I creep into your dreams
And see things as they are for you:

The hospital of sharpened knives
Where animals couple in greasy straw;

Where surgeons place a bawling child
Upon a slide toward the grave;

A body you must try to eat
That grows much larger with each bite,

Whose face you never see, although
You know full well it is your own.

You wake and say the world is good,
And spit its pips into my face:

I follow you, you follow me,
Across the fragrant earth's slow curve,

This solid shadow cast by God.
Whose world is this? Not mine, not yours.

This world of yours is black and white
And you are playing on its keys –

You think you make a rainbow world
Between the mindless sun and rain,

A perfect world with perfect flaws
But death has feet as well as hands

And plays your tune with awkward toes.
The music fills your room with lies,

You breathe them in and call them air,
Your heart forever out of time.

The keys are breaking into bud
While thorns appear along the stalk,

You say you live for paradise
And see the score within the wound,

But still it bleeds upon the keys
And paradise has roots in hell.

The sun is standing on your head,
Your shadow hides beneath your feet:

The music ends, and it is noon
With someone knocking on your door.

Don't worry so, the world is green
And there is sunlight on the stairs,

The four red chambers of the heart
Are all you need to make a life:

Your breaths do not require a home,
Your shadow does not ask for bread.

Don't sit and sharpen time's sharp claws,
Don't place your head inside its mouth:

Who knows if God will come to you
As fire, or as a woman's touch;

What does it matter if the soul
Is black on white or white on black –

The dead do not complain, they see
The roots of things abound with life.

Don't worry, put things out of mind,
Put all your sorrow and dark thoughts

Upon the dark side of the moon.
There is so much within your reach:

The sun's home in the honeycomb,
The quiet waters, the fragrant field.

Summers

The summer sky is overgrown, too large for the city;
By afternoon the heat has gone to seed
And heavy clouds mass somewhere over the ocean
Holding the capital in siege.
Trams shuttle by the river that twists and turns
Like someone unable to sleep,
Past small glazed hotels laced with iron verandahs
Where men in dark blue singlets sit and drink,
Overweight, as if pumped up from the navel.
Our garden is overgrown;
We sit and drink,
And smoke to keep away the first mosquitoes
That whisper for us to leave.

There is nowhere to go, and the long day
Stretches back, becomes a year, three years,
And finally never began at all.
Or if it did then here, now, as night comes slowly,
Following its shadow into the garden, under the almond tree.

A dozen years ago, in love for the first time,
I took a girl on a heaving, gearless council bus
To Wynnum, Brisbane's dusty Lido,
And sat all day
Upon a pier until her lips began to taste of salt.
We longed for water
And were two glasses of water, half-filled,
Pouring ourselves into the other,
Becoming tense, tenser, but never spilling.
The weight of borrowed money,
The deepening gaze of a Queensland afternoon,
And wanting to be older though never old.
It could not work,
And for a month we carried our love
Like an opened parachute dragging behind us,
The sky so large
As though the earth had shrunk in half.

Summer, nowhere to go, and yet
With the sound of chill water fanned upon leaves
I heard a dress lightly touching the long grass.
Beginning again, born far from home, and now another year
Is set down simply as a glass of wine when someone
Begins to talk, softly,
Of something new. Set down, put out of mind,
But without sadness, as though evening could possess
The garden in the quietest waves, naming us
Together in the one adventure of desire.
We sit and smoke,
Summer's riesling light now disappeared completely;
The murmur of passing traffic,
Heavy clouds effortlessly suspended above the sea.

The Companion

There is a man who will not let me sleep,
Each night he comes and trembles by my side.
He cannot be touched yet wind disturbs his hair,
He cannot touch yet shadows cover me.

Each night he comes and trembles by my side,
I reach towards him and he fades like day.
He cannot touch yet shadows cover me,
I hide within myself and he draws close.

I reach towards him and he fades like day,
I hear him though he does not speak a word.
I hide within myself and he draws close
And stretches out both arms as if in pain.

I hear him though he does not speak a word,
The sound of someone breathing, wind in trees.
He stretches out both arms as if in pain,
'I come to wound you and to heal the wound.'

Toscanini at the Dead Sea

The orchestra, a Parma garden in summer,
And music simply the desire for summer
In a world of winters: a century of Europe

Almost in love with death, the rotting fruit
Unable to fall, and careless smoke in eyes.
Think of the violin tuning, a young woman

Squeezing into the tightest silk dress,
The flute's notes like stones skipping water,
Puccinni dropping ash upon the keys.

How everything we love moves to one end,
Inevitable yet unexpected, a will to change
That somehow raises us above the end.

So it is right to find him here, at last,
Surrounded by water that refuses to live,
In the land where God was seen and almost caught

Like sunlight in a scoop of simple water,
This land where things reduce to the hard lines
Of light and dust, and make desire our home.

'Till Sotell Death Knoked at My Gate'

Don't let him think you're home: lock all the doors,
Cut off the telephone, and plug both ears;
Divorce your wife – she might make a mistake;
Let all your mail pile up outside; put out
Some bottles of rancid milk beside the gate.

You must let paint peel from the walls, and grass
Go troppo till it chokes the garden beds.
Ensure the lights won't work; a rat or two
Around the place will make the thing seem real;
A phoney grave in your front lawn might help

(But make sure it looks old, he's wise to that).
Forget your friends, tell them they've gone away,
And pray that they won't think to do the same:
This plan will only work for one or two.
Be scrupulous, the whole thing must look right,

Impeccable, if it will work at all.
Think of him constantly, and scratch his name
Upon your glasses so you won't forget;
Eat from a coffin lid, and sleep inside.
Be vigilant, he comes by all the time.

I almost forgot: check that he doesn't know
Your face already. Think if anyone
Has died inside your place: a father, child,
Or dog perhaps. Could he have seen you then?
If so, it's necessary you move at once.

You've got it all? Good, good. Now off you go.
Remember, if it fails you don't know me,
You don't know where I am: perhaps it's best
To say I went to live in Mexico.
We shall not meet again. Good luck my friend.

A Silver Crucifix on My Desk

Each day you wait for me,
Your arms
Raised as if to dive into my element,
Your bowed, precise body
Broken into the ways of earth. Someone
Has shrunk you
To a child's doll that I might understand
All that it is to be a man:
A simple cross
Where two worlds meet, a man
Caught there
And punished by the storm between two worlds,
A sword thrust into my desk
That tells me
With each new morning that the world
Will not escape
The world that we have made.
By evening
I no longer look your way, but watch
Your shadow
Steal toward my hand, I hear you talk
In the clock's dialect
And my pen
Becomes an ancient nail. How often
Have I turned from you,
How often
Have I tried to shrink you down
And wear you round my neck,
As safe
As any of the stars you made.
You stand
Amongst the things of this world,
Old letters, photos,
An ashtray and a wallet, the things
That come and go, but you
I cannot move.

Once,
I put you behind me, and all day
I felt your long, torn look
Upon my back. So you returned
To watch me
Answer letters, light cigarettes,
And place my books
Beneath your feet. Each year
I grow
Toward your age,
A face moving to a mirror,
I measure
Myself against you, a child
Beside his father,
But I go up and down, while you
Remain
Always above me, poised
With arms outstretched, ready
To dive
In this cold ocean
With its lost treasure,
Its gorgeous fish, all blind as jewels,
Gliding through the darkness.

The Last Day

When the last day comes
A ploughman in Europe will look over his shoulder
And see the hard furrows of earth
Finally behind him, he will watch his shadow
Run back into his spine.

It will be morning
For the first time, and the long night
Will be seen for what it is,
A black flag trembling in the sunlight.
On the last day

Our stories will be rewritten
Each from the end,
And each will end the same;
You will hear the fields and rivers clap
And under the trees

Old bones
Will cover themselves with flesh;
Spears, bullets, will pluck themselves
From wounds already healed,
Women will clasp their sons as men

And men will look
Into their palms and find them empty;
There will be time
For us to say the right things at last,
To look into our enemy's face

And see ourselves,
Forgiven now, before the books flower in flames,
The mirrors return our faces,
And everything is stripped from us,
Even our names.

Poem to the Sun

Waking in a place without air,
    in this old house with its stick legs
And sunken furniture, cupboards
Of useless clothes, a coil
    smoking in the exhausted heat;
The feeling of weight,
    of wading through warm water;

You are already here
    before I wake, inciting the insects,
And making the windows sweat. Outside,

Lank plants with floating tendrils,
    everything magnified
As under water, the colours of spiders, snakes –
And you
    flowering on their thick flesh.

There are days
I have seen you returning, melting the late stars,
    then entering on your knees
To speak first to the grass, before
    climbing the tallest trees
To watch our fishbowl world:

I look at you
    and think of honey, tobacco,
Clean wood that splits and shows you there.
Sometimes I have wanted
    to lean upon you, before I see
I am within you
    and all this dust is you. My lord,

The sleepless have longed for you all night
And finally seen you
    exulting like a runner who sees the track;
Yet others distrust you,
You enter their rooms cautiously, a hand in cold water.

I have found you
    singing, dancing, in the knife before it cuts
And in the apple's white.
On heavy afternoons, when the city
    feels sealed in plastic,
I have found you resting
    in the creases of the river;

(And I have found you
    before the people wake, at work
In my black rooms, drawing the darkness
Out of each thing,
    and you above it all, your arms still opening).

III

1984-1990

And he said, Let me go, for the day breatheth.

What, said Jacob, art thou a thief, or a dice-player,
that thou art afraid of the day?

He replied: I am an angel, and this is my first turn
since my creation to sing praises.

CHULIN

Gypsophila

Another day with nothing to say for itself –
Gypsophila on the table, a child's breath
When breath is all it has to name the world

And therefore has no world. It must be made:
Her shadow sleeping on the wall, the rain
That pins fat clouds to earth all afternoon,

A river playing down the piano's scales.
This is the strangest of all possible worlds
With foam upon the beach, the sea's dead skin,

And lightning quietly resting in each eye.
Like gypsy camps or love, it must be made,
Undone, then made again, like the chill rain

That falls without hope of climbing back,
Content to leave its mark, for what it is,
Upon the window or in the child's mind.

Gypsophila on the table, rain outside,
The child will tune the world to her desire
And make another world to keep in mind:

These breaths of air in which we softly wrap
The rain's glass stems to let them fall again
In sunlight, or flower for ever in the mind.

A world of things with nothing at all to say,
A margin that absorbs our silences:
The child must take the lightning from her eye

And place it in the sky, her shadow must
Be told to fall asleep. This strangest world
In which we say *Gypsophila, Baby's breath* –

Gacela

There is the sunlight tangled in your hair
And there are soldiers sleeping with their guns.
'This viper, the world!' Teresa cried, and yet

I want the mango's wealth of juice, the stream
That makes the bird a fish and then a bird;
I do not want the desert's cayenne dust

And statues fighting in the city square.
The chambers of the heart are splashed with blood;
The soldiers toss and turn all night: I want

The road to stop its lazy morning stroll
And lead me straight to you, I do not want
The storm to crack its knuckles overhead

And do its imitation of a war.
At night the student slips past Caligula
While dreaming of Cleopatra's hands and hair

Then sees the asp reflected in her eyes –
I want the road that leads the soldiers on
To double back and tie itself in knots,

I want the bird to catch the stream's creased skin
And fly away with it, I do not want
The soldiers turned to stone by what they see.

'It's not so bad,' Teresa said, 'with just
A single night to spend in this foul inn' –
I want to spin the chambers of the guns

And make the bullets giddy in the air,
I want the snake to shed its skin and fly,
I want to feel the sunlight in your hair.

Firm Views

Back to the things themselves: this empty glass
With no idea of water; sleeping cats
That dream of ancient Egypt in the sun;

And ivy on the porch. Now leave the mind
With its divisions training on the page
And walk out through a world untouched by thought

Where things exist as things, not otherwise –
Impossible, the land is occupied
By things as they appear to sight and touch;

The mind approaches with its golden frame
And frames itself: a judge with balding wig
Who sentences himself without appeal

To life and death. The stone describes the peach,
The noisy bird that bends the branch and eats,
The sunlight bathing in the lazy stream,

And these describe the stone. The door is locked,
The windows covered with reflecting glass,
The landscape is a portrait of the mind.

That big clawed hammer rusting in the shed
Stands for the world: you grasp pure sullen weight
Not an idea; the handle scrapes your skin,

A signature of pain to make its point.
Just so. The hammer needs the hand that needs
A world of thought: the judge's hammer strikes

The bench, the sentence is, as always, jail
From which there can be no escape till death:
The judge is silent, standing in the dock.

Approaching Sleep

Footsteps in the attic, those crooked sounds
You hear at night, the train's blind whistle or
Dead letters slipped beneath your bedroom door,

And still there is your heart that beats upon
Your ear and fills you as you lie in bed;
It beats and beats but cannot keep good time

And lets it drip like water from a tap.
You write a letter of complaint to God
While half asleep, forgetting the address.

Outside, the night is wide as a winter lake
After the heavy rains, and it is June
With days that open like a Chinese Box.

If anything is real it is the mind
Approaching sleep, listing the tiny bones
Within the ear: *anvil, stirrup, hammer...*

The surgeon placed them on a woman's watch,
The seconds crudely sweeping underneath.
Within the ear, a fine Dutch miniature

With cool canals, a blacksmith by his horse,
A small boy playing on a smaller drum,
Old women who darn their shadows again each dusk.

There is a monster in the labyrinth
But still behind you, walking when you walk:
It is too late to get out now, the watch

You hold up to your ear stopped long ago;
That angry letter you wrote to God returns
Addressed to you, but now means something else.

The Ship

Nothing but rag and bones, the ship first wraps
The struggling knees and elbows of the wind
Then fills them out into a woman's curves

And leaves a woman running down the beach,
Her footprints chasing after her for hours.
So hot, the horizon lazes on the sea

Or winds itself up tightly in a shell.
The afternoon extends to the horizon
But suddenly you're half a lifetime old:

There is the ship, quiet as a butterfly,
With everywhere to go; and here you are
Left to yourself and bored, like that Greek girl

Who never could escape the labyrinth,
Found it when walking by the shore, in shells
Preoccupied with all the same old truths,

Something to do with loss, with being lost,
In any case with finding oneself alone
And still in love. The afternoon wears out

Its endless patience, watching all this blue,
Wears in its pointed shadows on the beach.
It's late, you are alone – the fact sinks in

And settles at the bottom of the mind
With other sundry bits of information.
How did that story end? You can't recall,

You watch the evening stars now coming out
Above the shrinking ship, a blackened gull
Still struggling over the horizon line.

That Bad Summer

Vast cobwebs in the sky. No wind for months.
Airports deserted, and the trains on strike;
Odd bits of cargo litter Lygon Street

Beneath a Fokker hanging by a wing.
A fierce silence everywhere you go:
Suburbs and parks crisscrossed by shade all day;

Your childhood dream of camping out in tents
All summer long has just about come true,
Though kids are kept inside on sedatives.

The air gone thick and bad. Some days it takes
An entire afternoon to cross a road,
Some days an hour to wink at one you love.

What's worse, the hottest year this century!
Our bedroom windows have begun to sweat,
Reflections in mirrors cannot stay awake,

While numerals peel off the Town Hall clock.
Better, perhaps, to sleep the summer through.
No longer shocked, good citizens lie down

Beneath skylights, observing spiders mate –
A blue movie curving round our sky;
Or watch that regiment attack the webs,

Ballooning past grey clouds with guns and knives.
Nothing much happening in parliament
Yet food supplies, I know, are running thin.

And here he comes again, that little man
With a bald patch, still puffing door to door,
Intently peddling jars of human breath.

Haranguing Death

Don't hide. I've had my eye on you for years
And let me tell you straight, you're *tedious*.
You've made your point, effectively at times,

But go quite overboard: those endless wars
And gaudy diseases! And when there's nothing else
You're staring from my new electric clock,

Forever playing patience with marked cards
Or ticking over like a taxi fare.
I bet it's you who puts those varicose veins

In ancient cheeses, nothing's too trivial!
I hope people all over the world agree
To have both legs chopped off before the end

Just so their graves are small. In fact, I hope
They open bottle shops in cemeteries
And hold outrageous parties so you can't sleep,

And people come to funerals, half-pissed,
In *Life Be In It* T-shirts! You – a king?
Don't be absurd! A decent crown would fall

Over your skull and rattle round your neck.
Besides, you smell – and haven't done a thing
About it for, well, centuries at least.

Your manners are appalling, shoving past
The queuing years, and all those epitaphs!
(You really haven't any taste at all),

Your column in the paper lacks all style
(I can't see how you ever got the job)
And, worse, your jokes are bad, close to the bone.

Winter at Pt Henry

Sharp winter in the marshes, vagrant wind
Cornered in trees fused black by sudden rain,
Clouds slowly leaking from the factories –

Tired habits of a landscape drained of point
Or pushed to an extreme: dead cartridges,
Damp mattress roots, the candid cries of gulls

From random treetops. It is late afternoon,
Small boats tethered to the bay's green smells;
Flies, quick as eyelids, blinking on the stream

As waves spread out their plunder on the sand.
The sun says zero firmly, used to loss,
And jettisons its cargo in the sea.

Evening dissolves the factories, the gull
Becomes his curdling note, and the wind
Has made a zither from the pylons' wires –

A grieving older than its instrument,
Outside the jurisdiction of suave minds.
This is the music played upon chill flesh,

The spirit's winter fascination, its thrill
That freezes, as a finger sticks to ice.
This is the skeleton key to every heart:

The tree becomes a branch, and then a twig
That feels its way in darkness like a root.
The pylons burgeon into ziggurats,

With evening around you, everywhere,
Its ancient strata finally exposed,
And cars are passing there, beneath night's cliff.

Facing the Pacific at Night

Driving east, in the darkness between two stars
Or between two thoughts, you reach the greatest ocean,
That cold expanse the rain can never net,

And driving east, you are a child again –
The web of names is brushed aside from things.
The ocean's name is quietly washed away

Revealing the thing itself, an energy,
An elemental life flashing in starlight.
No word can shrink it down to fit the mind,

It is already there, between two thoughts,
The darkness in which you travel and arrive,
The nameless one, the surname of all things.

The ocean slowly rocks from side to side,
A child itself, asleep in its bed of rocks,
No parent there to wake it from a dream,

To draw the ancient gods between the stars.
You stand upon the cliff, no longer cold,
And you are weightless, back before the thrust

And rush of birth when beards of blood are grown;
Or outside time, as though you had just died
To birth and death, no name to hide behind,

No name to splay the world or burn it whole.
The ocean quietly moves within your ear
And flashes in your eyes: the silent place

Outside the world we know is here and now,
Between two thoughts, a child that does not grow,
A silence undressing words, a nameless love.

Dispute at Sunrise

It is enough, this world, more than enough:
Plum blossom shivering along a branch,
The sun still hanging from a lemon tree,

The garden laced with frost. Dig for an hour,
You'll find Athens beneath Jerusalem –
The day begins without a push from God.

Clouds gather in the afternoon, rain falls
In detail and at large, as is its way;
The sour winds of summer begin to stir

Though far from here: in cities wild with heat
Cicadas shake maracas through the night
And make the sleepless sprawl beneath their sheets

Or walk in moonlight close as a lover's breath.
There are old mirrors fattening all day
On things that come and go, but midnight proves

The clock's hands are scissors in slow motion,
The spider will be trapped in its own web.
Pushed to one side, the mind becomes extreme

And cultivates a glasshouse world. Strange things
Breed in the margins of your prayer books:
Tall knights afraid of snails, a grunting bull

That milks a naked woman, monkeys dressed
In doctors' coats with glinting knives in paws –
Birds spoil the unripe fruit, and darkness finds

Its foothold in the shadow of a child;
It is enough, this world, but even now
The lemon tree is hanging from the sun.

Lullaby

Sleep, little one, now that the house is still
And evening arrives on crickets' legs:
It's hot, I know, and how the body weeps –

The mind is lumpy with hot things of day
But now the jasmine opens, your sheets are cool,
And sleep is quietly calling you by name.

'We're armed for peace,' the politician states,
Then leans out, smiling vastly, from the screen
To hold you in his arms. 'Sleep now,' he says,

'And then tomorrow all this world is yours'.
But he is tired, it seems, and starts to yawn:
He counts bombs falling as he falls asleep.

Sleep now, the jasmine blooms, and when night cools
The crickets rub their wings to keep you warm:
Let moonlight start to wash the dirty world

And try, again, to make things black and white.
The politician warms a brandy, counts
As missiles jump the moon, but cannot sleep.

The jailor, weeping, passed Socrates the cup,
'The good man has no fear of death,' he said;
And Hegel in Jena, standing on his head,

Could see the Spirit push French cannon wheels,
Disaster blossoming above the field.
While Athens rots, men walk upon the moon,

And brandy, like Napoléon, can make
Europe go swinging round in empty space.
Sleep, little one, it's time for you to sleep.

The Story

Enter the story here: their battle lost
And foreign soldiers digging as rain falls
Or doodles on truck windscreens half the night.

A nearby town hangs weightless from the moon;
Its Church's shadow gulps a street, its priest
Still looks for God as through a telescope.

Or here: while girls in frothing dresses spin
Across a room, caught in the music's arms.
A year before or after, hard to say.

The border bathes within a river, hangs
Between two trees, straight as a bullet's path.
Now watch the hero carefully growing up:

He holds his future as the air holds light,
He dips a pen into his mind and writes.
While dreams italicise his hopes and fears

He sews his name into his country's flag.
And see him here, at forty, at his peak,
The future closer now, but flat and strange

Like favourite clothes pegged tight upon a line.
The border must be moved, he tells his men,
It must be pushed right out to meet the sea.

He hammers them to uniforms and guns.
He threads a needle with unravelling thread.
The day begins on time. It knows that much.

Day arches its back, and thunderclouds appear;
A wind goes bragging round dark cornered rooms,
Their curtains bulging with the coming change.

The Map

The maps of death get better every day –
Young draughtsmen use a scale of one to one
With instruments that speed across a page.

So there's no need to hang around old graves
In black jeans, looking for a shady deal:
A simple map will tell you all you want.

You'll find a dozen in your corner shop.
I've heard it takes two trees to make each map,
Upsetting the environment, they say,

But people barely wait until they're home,
Unfolding sections on their lounge-room floor.
'Now where's the legend?' Father thinks aloud,

'Until we find the legend,' he expands,
'We can't tell if it's right-side up or not.'
It spreads into the kitchen, covers beds,

Then flaps out on the mail-box and the lawn...
Its creases are as sharp as Father's shirt.
'Beats me,' says Father, taking up his pipe

And rattling silver as he walks away.
'There's Uncle Harold!' Mother points, then goes
To make some coffee while the children stare

And play at generals, sticking in small flags.
'We'd best put it away now,' Mother says,
'Before Grandfather comes to see the kids.'

But already they've forgotten how it folds;
They try this way, then that. The map is vast
And all the neighbours help, but it won't close.

'This Stone Is Thinking of Vienna'
(Rudolf Carnap)

This stone is thinking of Vienna – so,
Why shouldn't it? That's better by a mile
Than thinking of Rudolf Carnap! After all,

Compare his *Aufbau* with the Belvedere
And then – be honest – put a price on each.
They're both baroque, it's true, but only one

Looks out across the Danube flowing by.
Vienna's where Mozart worked for half his life;
It's been a site of human habitation

Since Neolithic times! And I see why,
What with the Schönbrunn and the Stephansplatz.
No wonder stones think of it all the time,

I know I do! Ah, city of terraces
And Vienna coffee – those warm autumn days
Spent kicking leaves. You'll find a left-bank there

Like Brisbane and that other place, yes, Perth!
St Stephen's nave is *ninety-five* feet high –
What more do you desire? Fine music, art,

It's all there, but you'll have to fight your way
To see the Winter Palace, past all those stones!
In Vienna statues set their marble wigs

At rakish angles, and waltz beneath the stars –
What, is that Mozart on the radio?
That's proof enough for me. My bags are packed:

It's midnight now, I know, but afternoon
In Austria! The cabbie slams his door
And lifts my suitcase, 'What you got here, stones?'

'The Present King of France Is Bald'
(Bertrand Russell)

The present King of France is bald, alas,
And someone's spiked poor Sophie's cheese soufflé.
Wherever you look, the world has gone to pot:

A decent moustache cup can't be bought these days
For love or money; people walk around
With cats strapped to their wrists, trying to tell

The time of day by looking in their eyes.
The Book of Revelation's selling well
On fiction and non-fiction lists; and, yes,

The deserts are full of anchorites on stilts.
In fact the Church is running out of space
And trades tiaras for blocks of wilderness:

'New penitents must bring their *own* sand now,'
The Vatican decrees, 'and sackcloth too,
'Our former vast supplies are at an end.'

On horseback in Russia, Napoléon saw his troops
Sprawled out across the snow, some eating it,
Some using slaughtered horses for warm tents.

It turned his hair quite grey, and isn't it true
That doctors found some arsnic in his scalp?
It makes you think; but war is different now,

A matter of talks and maths: a switch is pulled
And particles perform their arabesques.
Like everyone else, I know just what went on:

How that cloud rose up like a mad soufflé,
And how those shadows ran into a wall,
How the Hiroshima survivors lost their hair.

'The Philosophy of Furniture'
(Edgar Allan Poe)

I'm sorry Madam but it's as I feared –
There's not a single rawhide bookcase left.
We've little call for Eskimo designs:

Wet caribou fur, you'll find, has had its day,
The same with walrus tusks; and 'Bering Sheets',
Though of the finest ice, once *à la mode*,

No longer sell at quite their former rate.
Ivory headrests too are out of stock:
After the five days' war there was a surge,

But pillows rallied and simply won the day.
Ashtrays on giraffe legs? Let me just check.
No, still awaiting fresh supplies alas –

Our African distributor's quite tied up
(Some trouble in Entebbe, so I'm told)
But perhaps Madam has not seen our range

Of imitation medieval thrones? Oh, please,
Do try one: that's the *Beowulf* design,
Just in from Denmark – very sturdy oak,

And this week only, an axe is thrown in free.
I'm sorry, Madam, it just fell from my hand!
Please, allow me; there, only the barest graze.

Now let me show our new, extensive line
In conversation chairs, *les caquetoires*,
Ideal for guests. Or perhaps Madam prefers

Iron maidens? This one is quite a favourite,
Inlaid with tortoise shell or mother-of-pearl.
Gift wrapped? Of course. Will that be cash or charge?

American Journal

Some days America is a state of mind
And you are sailing through the Caribbean,
A distilled blue that goes straight to the head;

Small boys go swimming there, naked as sunlight,
While wind-chimes tinkle like the finest rain
On warm verandahs of Chateaubelair

Where French girls take coffee and honey cake.
In Mexico the poor wait hunched in streets,
Weary as dust, with nothing to eat but light;

There are lizards with the hard eyes of God
That never close, and vases put aside
To collect virgins' tears. Some days the mind

Retreats into the body, feeling its way
Towards your heart, then stretches like a cat
Before a fire. But elsewhere, in New York,

Money sleeps in banks, in deep cool vaults,
Manhattan's skyline charting profit and loss
Above astrologers and bagel shops,

The quick faces of men with cuban heels.
Magnolias and jessamine down south
And negroes resting in a billboard's shade;

Yet even in Columbia's dark slums
Moonlight comes free, and you can stroll outside,
The hot air tasting faintly of watermelon,

And drink in that party half a block away –
Someone splashing out cheap wine, another
On saxophone, all making lazy jazz.

The Pleasure of Falling Out of Trees
(for Emily Kratzmann)

Grown ups do nothing but talk and drink all day
When – you know how it is – warm afternoons
Are simply made for falling out of trees

And all you need is someone to hold you high.
There are thick books just begging to be read,
Conflicting views about the State to ponder,

And endless fashions in clothes and French cuisine
That must be taken seriously one day.
But all of that can wait, at least for now,

Since something ought be left to fill the years
From nine to ninety-five or thereabouts,
And falling out of trees doesn't take much time,

Two seconds really (depending on the tree)
Yet somehow promises everything to come:
The pavement crazy with the shadows of birds,

A rush of blue, some goosebumps on your arm,
The smell of lemons mingling with rich heat.
There must be more than this, I know, and yet

If we could only trust that utter freedom,
That falling like spring rain, we would come close
To what it is. And laying down our talk

We could live quietly with one another –
Not worrying whether the clock might be made
To wipe its hands of all our yesterdays,

But simply watching sunlight in the trees
Or listening to the beat of the gulls' wings
And being happy, nothing to squander but time.

Winter Rain

(in memory of Vincent Buckley)

Two weeks after the funeral, and yet
I catch myself reaching for the phone,
About to dial your number. God in heaven,

What will it take for me to realise
That you aren't there? Your photograph, perhaps,
Stuck on the kitchen cupboard, and several years.

I used to think that death was some dark thing
That followed people round. You taught me this,
In dying, that it's human, almost shy.

This fraying collar, that hair upon my sleeve –
Neither has anything to do with you,
Yet now I'm strangely tender toward them

As though in death you took me by the hand
And turned me to a larger, calmer world
Where everything is loved for what it is.

I want to stay here, in this other world,
A moment longer – caught in a ray of light
With only dustmotes floating up and down,

I want to be at peace, accepting loss,
And feel that you're now home, like winter rain
That falls all day upon its mountain stream;

When suddenly that old poem comes to mind
(One that I never cared for until now)
Where Tu Fu writes to his dear friend Li Po,

Regretting the distance that separates them,
And wondering when they will meet again
And argue verse over a cask of wine.

The Letter

They had it last, I hear, around the Court:
A clerk was observed fingering the cord,
And someone was called in to testify

Whether the seal bespeaks a chancellor
Or bishop – the experts disagree, it seems,
Something about a star or fleur-de-lis –

And on the News we saw it up quite close:
A scientist sighed, then put the letter down
(Her cigarette was lying on a bench –

A breeze came in and took a cheeky drag).
Nobody knows how old it really is
Or where it's from, yet even soapies break

For news updates when anything is heard.
'My dear one, listen to me now…' it starts,
Though scholars contend that's a later hand

And hear the author's voice much later on,
With 'If I left you (but I won't)' or even
'As if you had forgotten everything…'

Found in a chest, a cell, a Papal desk?
The Government will not commit itself,
While thousands link it with a UFO.

Corrupt or not, the letter works non-stop;
Each reader thinks it's somehow meant for him.
(Nobody here has slept these past few days:

Nights see us drafting marvellous replies,
Though no one knows who he is writing to
And only the wind drops by to read a line.)

Peniel

Someone is whispering my name tonight.
Not here, although a radio sings the Blues
So softly you could almost hear a breath;

Not here, where moonlight chills the lemon tree
And makes a warmth out of the simplest touch.
My mother is dead: I have no name, and so

She quietly sings to me all day all night,
A name I never heard till now, a name
She whispered months before I was born.

My name is quiet as a fingerprint –
It makes no trouble, it tells me who I am,
I've seen it often. And yet, I don't know why,

These past few months I brood on Genesis,
Those stories like a rainbow at evening,
And find them all too true. At thirty five,

All those I love have passed by Peniel,
And everyone longs to take another name,
And everyone knows a blessing is a wound,

And yet, what help is that? I do not know;
Those stories tell me nothing but themselves:
At three a.m. I find myself asleep

Beside some tales I hardly half-believe,
And doze again, as hearing my name sung,
A name no one has ever called me by,

Half me and half a child I never was –
My mother's child.
                        I wake sometime round four
And find the moonlight sleeping on my cheek.

Making a Rat

I forget everything, and make a rat.
With little ambition at first, an amateur,
I try a roof rat – grey, long tail, sharp ears –

But with a will that staggers the human mind.
For months I labour on those teeth, that jaw
With strength enough to gnaw through beams of wood;

For years on end I fiddle with those ears
That make the lowest noises stand erect.
I give up dinners, seminars and sex

To breed the things it carries in its mouth –
Those strains of typhus, rabies, fever, plague.
I give up sleep for weeks to make its eyes

That pierce the darkness as I slowly work.
All day the mind will multiply itself
Just dreaming of a whisker hanging right,

A foreleg muscle tensing for a leap.
My mother dies, my father turns to drink,
And churchbells grow threadbare warning me;

And then one day the postman brings a book
Wrapped in brown paper, without card or note:
One Hundred Reasons Not to Make a Rat.

I put in longer hours, buy classy tools,
But still the rat won't work. I'll try again –
This time a Norway rat, eight inches long,

And from today I'll get it right from scratch.
I have my knives, my books, a practised hand.
Don't worry about that, I'll get it right.

The Historian of Silence

The historian of silence casts no vote.
The polling booth, he finds, is always closed,
His name not on the roll. He pays a fine,

And likes the feel of bank notes in his hands.
Perhaps no one has ever written well
About big money: how the mouth goes dry

When dreaming of it, how it slips past Jags
And teenage prostitutes alive on smack
While lacing them together in advance.

And no one bothers much about those things
That never hit the papers: tart, thin smells
Of boiling overalls on Sunday walks,

Or how, last war, French country girls would keep
Bright slabs of butter wrapped in cabbage leaves,
Or how a word can sting you like a wasp.

All this attracts a historian of silence:
He sees the grand equation's heart, that x
Permitting everything to show itself,

And knows that he must amplify its beat.
His only instruments are lucid prose
And noisy friends with views on everything.

Nothing goes right for years: papers are lost,
A marriage sours, and ideas start to fray.
And then, one winter's afternoon, he writes

That bold, divisive opening paragraph
(The one his favoured students quote too much).
His pen moves silently across the page.

The Black Telephone

An old black telephone rings in the dark.
How far away it is, when heard asleep,
Somewhere across a border, in the hall;

How far away, and if I answer it
My life will shape itself around a voice.
Such darkness as before God spoke a word,

And no one should be calling at this hour.
The names of things creep out into the night
But all creation tenses round that phone.

It is the Duke of Cumberland, breathing hard,
'Where are you? Leave for Culloden Moor at once!'
I do not want to answer. I know him well,

Let all the drumming stay in 'Forty-Six,
With all the sleet, with all the filthy snow.
Let famous generals rot in their gilt frames.

It is my mother, awake in Brisbane's heat,
Announcing the anniversary of her death.
I do not want to answer. Go to sleep,

I know those stories better than myself:
Old relatives who smell of photo albums,
The knotted streets of Leeds where I was lost.

The night is black and full of secret truths;
It wants to tell us something urgently
And has been trying hard for many years:

An emptiness that longs to talk to you,
And say, 'Well, first you must do this, then this...'
But still that telephone rings in the dark.

Reading at Evening

The day is heavy, dragged down by the sun
That looks into each window one last time
And finds old air now aching with the heat,

Windows becoming mirrors, and a clock
Still hedging bets with one hand here one there.
Soon only dark outside, as though the day

Disclosed its one assumption at the end
When there's no time to argue about truth,
No common ground for talk: as with a man

Who finds the standard metre slightly short.
The house stands still and cracks its swollen joints.
There is a volume open on the desk

And inside proofs that books do not exist;
You sit it on your knees, its argument
A cat's thin eyes that pierce the liquid night,

Possessing a knowledge difficult to grasp,
As though it rested just behind the page,
Upon the silence before you touched the book.

A cat is sleeping on the cool verandah
Where a full moon looks down, boiled white as bone,
Now finely round, chastised all yesterday

In Paris by the standard metre that rests
Bathed in blue light, immaculate in glass,
A powerful relic of a martyred saint.

The book continues, brilliant to the end,
And then, at twelve, the clock adds its applause.
Outside, the cat is chasing its own tail.

The Gift

One day the gift arrives – outside your door,
Left on a windowsill, inside the mailbox,
Or in the hallway, far too large to lift.

Your postman shrugs his shoulders, the police
Consult a statute, and the cat miaows.
No name, no signature, and no address,

Only, 'To you, my dearest one, my all…'
One day it all fits snugly on your lap,
Then fills the backyard like afternoon in spring.

Monday morning, and it's there at work –
Already ahead of you, or left behind
Amongst the papers, files and photographs;

And were there lipstick smudges down the side
Or have they just appeared? What a headache!
And worse, people have begun to talk:

'You lucky thing!' they say, or roll their eyes.
Nights find you combing the directory
(A glass of straw-coloured wine upon the desk)

Still hoping to chance on a forgotten name.
Yet mornings see you happier than before –
After all, the gift has set you up for life.

Impossible to tell, now, what was given
And what was not: slivers of rain on the window,
Those gold-tooled *Oeuvres* of Diderot on the shelf,

The strawberry dreaming in a champagne flute –
Were they part of the gift or something else?
Or is the gift still coming, on its way?

IV

1991–1998

If I do not answer for myself, who will answer for me?
But if I answer only for myself, am I still myself?

ABOTH

The Dressmaker

One of those late summer days, flaring and still.
Brisbane idles outside, while the fan
Churns air all afternoon. One of those days
When good for nothing hours
Go by just carrying smells of cut grass.
Lightly, so lightly, they pass over you:
Hours stunned by heat
Creeping through drawn blinds;
And the feeling, as you hang around, of being erased.
One of those days that stick to you.

A useless sort of day, good enough for reading *Beano*
And staying home from school.
Yet I remember pins in mother's mouth, her neck
Bent to the Singer's needle, hands feeding
Bright cloth to the machine.
More bored than ill, I thumbed through *Burda*
And caught a passion for tailored skirts.
That night she had ten pick-ups on the books.
And every dress was finished;
Her watch, set fifteen minutes fast, made sure of that.

As if those minutes could be counted now
Like pennies in a jar: *Good God,*
I've ten full years here kept aside!
I walk around her empty house – it's just the same –
And feel old February heat
That slobbers over you for hour on hour.
Nothing to do, I sit the evening out
On her verandah: wisps
Of grass smoke rising way above the power lines,
A car radio turned low somewhere near.

The Carpenter

Dark room,
You make me see it, even now:
A hint of planes and chisels, hammers all strung up,
Blond curls of wood,
And everywhere the faint, fine tang of oil
And pipe smoke: a deep smell
Of London, 1963.

Don't go, old man,
Straight-backed in your forbidden shack
Built out of bits and pieces of leftover night,
Don't go, not now
You've come this far. Who else will give
The sinister coins of the desert? Who
Will find men lost in a map's crease?

Grandmother told me,
Just once, she saw you standing near her bed
When you were out in Egypt.
But you said nothing,
And once more you are in the dark
With not a word to say,
With my heart pounding like quick hammer blows,

Eyes widening to catch the light,
What light there is in this late memory of you,
Strong, massive and alone out there
In that old night:
A nail between your teeth,
Your left hand resting on the vice's grip,
A dented hammer raised to strike.

The Glorious Age

The schoolroom is on stilts, and you can sometimes feel a breeze stroke your legs, wafting up through cracks in the floorboards. It is still the age of inkwells and metal nibs in Brisbane, the age of sweaty hands on blotting paper, the great and mighty age of 'Copy Book', the glorious age of parsing which will never end, our teacher tells us, we will never see the sun begin to set on that, no, not in his lifetime or ours. Grammar belongs to Wednesday afternoons, when the clock dozes a little and lets an extra ten minutes slip in each hour, when Lucy the top girl goes to the locked cupboard in the corner, gathers the books and hands them out, row by row. Each page is faintly ruled in blue, and while we clean our nibs Mr Smith is slowly writing sentences on the blackboard, melodious sentences I cannot understand, long sentences he loves from books on his 'special shelf': Addison and Gibbon, Hume and Chesterfield. '...As the Monks were the Masters of all that little Learning which was extant', he writes, breathing heavily, 'and had their whole Lives entirely disengaged from Business, it is no Wonder that several of them, who wanted Genius for higher Performances, employed many Hours in the Composition of such Tricks in Writing as required much Time and little Capacity...' No breeze today, only cicadas and nibs scratching. 'Now boys', he says, 'find the auxiliary verb in the first sentence, and draw a mango over it. And girls, I want you to find the indirect object – yes, Pam, that same sentence – and draw a pear over the top (yes, use your coloured pencils).' Soon there are bunches of black grapes clustering over main verbs, a fine ripe pineapple spiking a noun phrase, two or three small tangerines nestling in an ellipsis, and a subject almost hidden by dangling dates. It is the age of wicked heat, of parents who whisper in bed at night, the age of broken marriages, of teachers with bottles of booze in drawers, the age when boys are caned for not knowing subject from predicate, a Cavendish banana from a Gros Michel. The grammar book grows heavy with tropical fruit; Addison stares out the window, longing for the cold air of London; while Smithy takes another swig behind the blackboard, muttering, 'Damn kids don't know nothing'.

Heat

A late November day, o lord, and a wild heat has taken root.
By noon those old iron sheds, just over the railway line,

Are blazing, and the young blokes mowing paspalum there
Have stripped to jeans and radio:

Heat strumming the horizon

And burnt air shimmering.

They lick it off their lips, they taste it in the grass stalks. Ah,
Sweet Jesus, how they love it, and they tell you so

In the way they wipe sweat off their foreheads
In the way they let it run straight down their cheeks.

I see the sun is vast and terrible
I see the gums are hanging down their leaves,

O lord, while dead grass screams and lashes air
And a young man plays a hose.

And it is good, recalling this from thirty years ago,
And letting it sing awhile:

That cut paspalum going up in flames

Those boys enjoying it.

Two crouching down now, pinching cinders with their thumbs,
Two standing up and stretching,

Then gone,

Just leaning back and smoking in the arse of a beat-up council ute,
Their tranny doing all the talking

As the city grows around them

And the heat, o lord,

The heat.

Drawing Room, Annerley, 1966

Thick vines and shutters, then the drawing room.
Within the gloom, a fern case – moss, a maidenhair,
A delicate Italian girl with long white legs –
Her mother's long ago:
                              carved emu eggs set high
On crystal vases; large gilt oils; old books;
Odd potted plants
And reeds beside the great bay window;
A cushion with a big embroidered cat

About to pounce. *Gouache, ottoman,*
Couverette and *Parian,*
                              we all learned silently,
And had to stay for lunch: *credenza, o credenza...*

                    *

(Outside, a crazy summer snarling on the lawn
And mother whispering
Of hands and words, of knives and forks;

And then, outside the whole encumbering day,
Another world
Unfolding with broad smells of jacaranda trees.)

                    *

As evening fell
The woman's son, just out from Wacol, strapped us in his Ford
And hit the Ipswich Road: Mount Coot-tha
A darkness hid in dark, the river
A rumour of deep mud and party lights,

My parents holding hands back home to the hostel
While catching up
On years and years of Annerley,

And mother talking ottomans and emu eggs,
And father saying *Yes* and *Yes,*
And the big highway with its white line curving up ahead...

Her Name

Poincianas flared that Christmas holiday.
They grew right up against the flyscreen wire,
Over verandahs, living off wet heat,
That heavy Brisbane heat that knocks you flat

And hangs around all night, outlasting beer,
A heat that bruises souls. I saw them burn
Outside my bedroom screen while thunder rolled:
Thin petals flickering. All summer long

I'd sit up late, half-cocked for an exam,
Far off, but waiting there like Judgement Day;
And, thick with work and beer, sink down to sleep
In a frayed circle of light. But often, though,

I'd fantasize about a girl from school,
And sometimes call her up, late, very late.
She'd sent me in the mail one steamy day
A picture of Our Lady: on the back

A scarlet lipstick kiss signed 'You Know Who'.
Some nights I'd walk the darkness of our house
And take a needle from my mother's room
And slowly, making love by telephone,

Inscribe her name on petals, sharp and red,
And feel the needle cut through tiny veins.
The whole of summer passed through every night
And smouldered in the letters as they formed,

And everything she was and I could be
Seemed darkly written there and not in books:
A love to grow with us and judge us both,
A fire I felt when whispering her name.

No Easy Thing

Angels of summer live closest to the earth
And know the joys of late November days.
No easy thing, my friend, to sense the thrill
Of mouth on mouth and not to have it now;

To see a breeze, right off Deception Bay,
Amaze a man who's lived an afternoon
Abandoned to the heat... If sunlit minds
Can gaze at earth and almost feel desire,

What hope for us? Thin days and stunted days
Unnoticed in the summer's rage for love,
When, once or twice, an angel will descend
And quietly come toward you all your life:

He has a word to whisper, one that heals,
But crazed cicadas start to shake the night.
No easy thing, I say, yet hardly know
Whether I mean an angel or the summer.

The Great Explorers

In those days maps were mostly full of blanks.
Someone had got the coastline vaguely right
And there were angels blowing hard at sea,
But 'Unexplored' was written everywhere.
Out west, train tracks were penciled on the sand.

The great explorers were always out on strike.
Men queued for hours to see them riding past
Or drinking hard in seamy Melbourne bars.
'Conditions are awful there,' Burke said to Wills,
'And bugger me who wants an inland sea?'

Nothing could get those clowns to move a foot.
One year the scent of roses kept them home,
And then a savage noise leapt from the dark.
Quite frankly other seasons were too hot:
Good shade, one time, cost fifteen bob a yard.

It was that very year, the Church proclaims,
Bad angels hocked their haloes for a beer;
That very year, just north of Watson's Bay,
Statues of George the Third were washed ashore.
They spoke when touched: 'I am not mad,' they said.

The laughter lasted the nineteenth century
But World War One soon put a stop to that.
The great explorers joined up, man and boy.
Back home, good people sang 'God save the King!'
And watched their maps drain down to purest white.

The Discoverers
(after René Char)

They came, men from the other side, woodsmen we didn't know,
      a clan we never name.
They came in numbers.
They appeared at the line that separates the cedars
From the old harvest field now watered and green.
They were hot after their long trek.
Their hats shaded their eyes and they slouched anyhow.
They saw us and stopped.
Plainly they hadn't expected to find us
On rich dark soil with fields all tightly ploughed,
Not worrying much who saw us.
We looked up and called them over.

Their spokesman uprooted himself, then another just as dazed.
We've come, they said, to warn you of a cyclone, a fearful one.
We don't know any more about it than you,
Only what we've heard in stories and from old folk.
But why are we so strangely happy here, like children again?

We thanked them and sent them home.
But first they drank, and their hands trembled, and their eyes
      laughed over the rims of cups.
Men of trees and axes, hard men, but poor at irrigating land,
      at building shacks and decorating them,
Men who wouldn't hear of winter gardens and the husbandry of joy.

Of course, we could have convinced them and won them over
For a fear of cyclones touches everyone.
And yes, a cyclone was about to hit;
But who'd waste breath by saying so and upsetting the future?
Where we are, days look after themselves.

After Sappho

Ah what a star, that boy,
The one who hangs around with you all day
And gazes in your dreamy eyes,

Half-breathing in that laugh
That goes straight to my head. You know,
I see you on a tram, and I just melt:

'You come here often?' (groan). I'm dumb,
Can't look you in the eye,
Can't stop my heart from pounding:

My stomach tightens, a prickly sweat
Runs down my back;
I blush like – like a stupid kid at school,

And might as well be dead.

Her Whisper

    Vertical day:
She simply whispered, 'I love you,'
And I walked home that afternoon
Down lanes I never tried before.

    I was a noun
Translated to a verb: how strange
To find the power to say 'I',
Yet never want a microphone;

    Though even here,
Near home, I was the smallest place
Where weird emotions found their way
Across the world to stay awhile.

    (And yet, you know,
I never was a word, only
A man, almost a man, at last,
And getting lost while walking home.)

Her Kiss

She said, 'I kissed another boy today.'
Well, that was thirty years ago, and I
Thought then, 'In time it will not hurt at all',

Imagining an afternoon with clouds
Somehow at peace in their high tiers of air,
An older man who goes about his work

Not worried much by silly girls, or who
He was on evenings when thunderstorms
Shook a strange sky until there was no light.

I look outside my office at the clouds
On the first day of summer: endless blue
Parades with white for me, and only me.

So where is 1968 these days?
That older man would know. Fool that I am,
I pick a wound until it starts to bleed.

.

The Letter

Just casting round for something good to read
On the train home, I riffle lovely names:
D'Annunzio, Gozzano, Montale... no,
There's *Lavorare stanca* – fancy that,
I haven't picked it up since, let me see,

Since 1980, fifteen years ago,
And here it is. Well, well, some grammar notes
On yellow paper; a mistaken verb;
And there beside my favourite line of all,
Another list of conjugations – no,

A letter written in a childish hand
I open then gulp down and down and down,
Something about 'regret' and 'loneliness',
Something about 'in ten years' time, maybe'.
I say *il mestiere di vivere*

But far too badly to impress myself.
I read those poems once again, and try
Ne stilla una pena antica.
Fifteen fine years have taught me 'peace' and 'calm'
Yet still a letter slaps me in the face.

The Room

It is my house, and yet one room is locked.
The dark has taken root on all four walls.
It is a room where knots stare out from wood,
A room that turns its back on the whole house.

At night I hear the crickets list their griefs
And let an ancient peace come into me.
Sleep intercepts my prayer, and in the dark
The house turns slowly round its one closed room.

The Book

A book is waiting for you in the dark:
    She placed it on your desk today,
An inch or two from where the light attacked,
Beside fresh jonquils dozing in their vase,
    Not far from pencils, knife and clips,

And other books that looked then looked away;
Before you thought, though very far from home,
    About soft toys spilt on the floor,
Before she thought about that boiling milk
Or stormclouds blowing in from Bordertown.

They came this afternoon, and now the sky
    Collapses hard upon your house.
Some months ago, in Västerås or Serres,
The book took breath and then set out for you.
    It smelled two oceans, then became

A choir of simple words that sang new worlds.
Now it is here; it sits upon your desk
    While day relaxes into night,
And dreams already of a long trip home,
Beginning when you hold it in your hands.

Your wife sits down and sips a magazine;
    Your girls call sleep, a shy old cat,
And fear the dark that hangs around your house;
And your true journey waits, an hour away,
    When all your bags are in the hall.

Dark Angel

It was the sound of darkness, mother said,
But still I heard you calling in the night.
It was our old poinciana, straight from hell,
Its full-moon perfume wafting through the house...

Or fine mosquitoes, rising from the river
Just coiling in the dark there, down the road;
It was that sound, of water and the trees,
That somehow found a way into my sleep.

At night, between poinciana and the river,
Something of me walked round and round and round
Near that black water with its snags and snakes
And long low sounds that keep the grass alive,

And you were there as well, a touch away,
Always about to pull the darkness back,
And there were always branches rustling hard
And tall reeds bending. Never any wind.

Thinking of David Campbell

That thick sweet smell of country gums in heat,
Leaves dangling down,
And small bright angels hanging high up there,

Asleep, I'd say, most of them, up in the piccolo branches,
With not a word to say,
And all of them just lazing there, light passing through their minds,

No sound from heaven,
No gold mouth opening, but the cicadas still intoning,
Light, heat, Monaro noon...

*

Angels have nothing much to say, except
'Exceed the picayune', meaning
Let warm summer light flow through the soul for hours on end;

The rest is rhythm, impromptu love: a long fantasia
We play deep down
While earthed in everyday address, that world

Where minutes paw the ground,
Where bread is bought and lyrics are composed
And old cicadas drone their mass.

*

Friendship will take strange freight on summer days like this,
Years after your dying
Has entered my body, and my body has changed,

Hot days and odd days, with grass seed flying,
Days flecked with death,
A lovely weight of hours from twenty years ago:

Late afternoon beside the lake, you reading new poems aloud,
Our lunch's wine still singing in my head,
And all the angels listening.

The Fragrance of Summer Grass

After being silent for the best part of a long hot day
The quiet will sometimes deepen
And the dog hours will slowly stretch themselves

And something inside relaxes too
As evening enters in its own sweet, fine and bluesy way,
And so it happens, once or twice,

An old friend passes by:
And as I speak it would be false to say he died
Some fifteen years ago,

It would be false to say a word, this one or that,
For there is no more than a scent
That touches me the moment it withdraws,

A fragrance of high summer grass:
And all I know is a great calm that deepens in his name
And take it as his gift.

We Must All Die

But no: I felt, just now, as though someone
Had cut away my last moment on earth,
And so I turned to the crab apple tree
In our back yard and asked how I should live

Now I will live for ever, and though the sun
Had only just laquered its dark leaves
That plant said nothing. Well, fuck you, I thought,
And bothered a mosquito passing by,

Hey you, who will so soon be underground,
Tell me how I should live, but it looked blank
And hummed that it was watched over too
And not to worry so. I stroked my cat

Who arched her spine and wonderfully declared
That she knew best. Shadows were thickening,
And then our ancient lemon tree out back
Went quiet, and the couch grass whispered no...

Brisbane

I travelled to a city made of heat
Where brown snakes slithered past a paw-paw tree.
Our new house stood on stilts and creaked at night
And thunder took the place of history.

Where brown snakes slithered past a paw-paw tree
I sat and wrote my future in a daze.
Huge thunder took the place of history
And yet a *no* uncoiled within each *yes*.

I sat and wrote my future in a daze:
And though the sun kept hammering my head,
And though a *no* uncoiled within each *yes*,
I listened hard for what is left unsaid.

And while the sun kept hammering my head
The bright hours took my body, one by one.
I listened hard for what is left unsaid,
Convinced it called to me from far within.

So dark hours took my body, one by one,
And played for all my future, all my past:
Convinced it called to me from far within,
I waited for a strangeness I could trust.

With all my future, and with all his past,
My father claimed that city made of heat.
I waited for a strangeness I could trust
In a house that stood on stilts and creaked at night.

The Voice of Brisbane

On summer evenings, when the ache of thunder
Enters your body and lightning prowls around
Saint Helena then streaks along the beach,

And when the day no longer knows its name,
And vegetates (the insects mostly drunk),
You sit and wait for rain to sack the town.

                    *

The hours get larger but you cannot sleep:
You walk around your house, inside the heat,
And listen for the silence of the night,

But there are raindrops falling out of time
Onto that concrete slab outside the window,
A breeze caressing bougainvillea,

Damp canvas slung across a flywire screen
And breathing. Hush now child, can you make out
The bamboo knotting in the tangled grass?

                    *

Astride Mount Coot-tha, raise both hands to God
And silence every car and bus and train.
Let midnight walkers count themselves to sleep.

Now listen for a cat upon the roof
And take away its mew, now place yourself
On Wickham Terrace, facing City Hall,

Subtract the motion of the clock's great hands;
There is a ferry riding Breakfast Creek –
The slap of wave on wood must be removed.

Cicadas are not to rub their legs tonight,
And brothels in the Valley will be closed.
The moonlight must not splash in pools of rain.

*

Yet still I heard a murmur in the quiet,
Lying in bed those summer nights, as though
All Brisbane were a shell against my ear,

A distant roaring somehow caught in calm:
The Voice of Brisbane, I would tell myself,
Though sensing, even then, that undertone

Was older than goanna and brown snake,
The lazy river mumbling in its sleep.
At nightime, in the hours between two words,

I heard that murmur sifting all I loved:
Nothing is lost, whispered the heart of things,
Or was it *Nothing lasts*? I could not tell.

The brash young morning would not give a view,
Absorbed already with its crazy heat,
Its whistles, sparking trams and lorikeets.

My Mother's Brisbane

My mother's Brisbane was a mess of frangipani and flame tree
Seen from the windscreen of her car
Travelling through suburbs whose names she could not say

It was odd nights that fell without the benefit of evening
While working on dresses for weekends she wouldn't see
And it was hours with nothing much to do

It was a city remembered from old migrant books
Something about eleven hills and thunderstorms
Something about the Walter Taylor Bridge

It was the *Tele* and the Ekka; it was thongs and togs;
It was a child with a heavy port
It was a monthly visit to the Queen Street Mall

Something to do with Tracey Wickham I remember now
And something to do with Kingsford-Smith
And Lady Cilento had a place as well

Boris the Black Knight was someone she had to live with
Though Wickety-Wak she didn't
And Pancake Manor she never saw or Bunya Park

But the humidity she felt
While bent over that Singer on a summer's day
Or puffing through a family afternoon at Fig Tree Pocket

And the westerlies she came to feel as well
As though she let the city enter her a little more each year
Until she gossiped about the ghost at Stanley Street

And once she saw a bearded dragon half asleep
Beside the pawpaw tree in our back yard
And grabbed a rolling pin and chased it down the drain

You

My mother taught me how to thread
A needle with frayed cotton, how
It must be licked then bitten hard.

For ten years now she's hardly moved
Inside her grave, and in that time
My life's unravelled more than once.

Some nights I've seen that needle's eye
And woken, knowing all too well
It was the moment of my death,

But now, these fine long summer days,
When you are lying in my arms
I know my soul must pass through you.

*

Odd moments in a magpie's song
That tell us things we cannot know
Until we are the bird we hear,

And young gray kangaroos asleep
Beside those mounds of half-baked earth
We almost thought were kangaroos:

It is a strange and nameless world,
This one which you have made for me,
A world created by your touch.

*

Four days before I kiss her mouth?
Dear God, please let my fingers ease
The valve you hide so well, the one
That keeps this world brimfull of time.

Membranes

1

A voice, almost a voice, in the wee hours
When no one else is home: a body turns
And feels its comprehension of the bed,
An ear affirms the silence of its house

And only then admits a pounding heart.
Heat sits in judgement over everyone,
O Lord, this summer night whose rising up
And going down give cruel sleep at best:

Each louvre set to catch the storm's cracked air
And old verandahs slung out round the back
All drenched with moonlight and mosquito nets.
Tough kids are fucking in the high school yard

While traffic whispers on the Ipswich Road;
A train bears empty carriages out west,
The river sighs while passing Mandalay.
There was no voice. That girl from years ago

Was not about to speak before you woke.
Ah, let her go. And let those other souls
With cold, fixed eyes of dolls left under beds
Go home, o let them slip into the dark...

A voice, almost a voice, though not a voice:
Something between the mind and night, perhaps,
Something that tries to speak but always fails
And leaves a memory with nothing there.

2

To walk all day beside the lazy river,
Beginning from its loop at Blackheath Road
And vaguely heading down to Cockatoo,
A full canteen of ice slung round my neck,

Then cutting back at four down bolted paths
That open, suddenly, onto thick bush
Or spiky fences running fast for miles
At Wacol Prison or the 'Private Road':

It was somewhere round there I lost my way,
Some Sunday when the mercury went mad,
And found a factory defunct for years
With grass that grew right through the broken glass,

And I remember climbing up and down
And gulping thick warm water with a taste
Of tin and leather from my father's war,
And I recall a sign that said 'CONDEMNED'

Through cobwebs, swastikas and clumsy hearts,
And red brick dust that ran beneath my nails
And loud mosquitoes ripping up my arms,
The walls all going wavy in the heat,

And none of it adds up to anything,
Only a nameless fear that sometimes leaps
From nowhere on these summer evenings:
Just coming to; no stars; a drip of blood;

The sweat already cold upon my back,
And drunken voices flapping in the wind,
And someone, me, now smashing through the bush
And leaving someone, me, still sleeping there.

3

Half-dreaming of desire, or solitude,
I thought, Apollo Bay: arriving there
One winter evening while driving west
And drinking dirty water from a hose

Then clambering around the breakwater
With a kind girl I didn't love enough:
The fishing ships at ease, a massive hill
Intent on brooding over all the bay

And moving closer, so it seemed, as night
Came home at last, but slowly, wave on wave.
Nowhere more beautiful than here, I thought,
(A sorrow old as all the stars was out

And roaming round the bay, as though it knew
Our bodies were both made of stars). No time
More radiant than now: her fingertips
Just touching near her mouth, and ocean waves

Returning once again in their good time
While I was nearly breathing her warm breath.
A moment that unfolds and makes a life,
A moment surely reaching out to – no,

Not that, I thought, not that, and then stepped back.
An icy breeze was on the loose, and so
'As Goethe said,' I said, and she agreed,
And there was somewhere else we had to go.

4

(*i.m.* G.H.)

The train is skimming Maryland at night
When you are called back home. But who? And where?
You look outside, and someone there looks back.
It's you, thank God, well almost – yes, it is,

And sleep belongs to someone else's life
And that was you as well, or nearly. No:
Old questions breathe beside you as you wake
And bring old answers slowly to their knees.

Snow falls on roads where you will never walk,
On trees that you will never sit beneath;
It was her face you saw out in the night
And she was whispering a word. Lost, lost,

Forever lost, and waves pass over you:
A mountain, and a wine glass being filled,
A long embrace and then a sudden look
That cancels years and years. Well it was her,

And so her dying enters into you;
After a year or more of clenching hard
At last it happens, all that void at once,
Its full enormous rush against the heart

With people all around awake, asleep,
Some counting minutes till they open doors
And others reading Bibles with a pen,
And no one here can take the truth away,

Not the conductor in his uniform,
Not the dark face that looks at you outside.
O let her go the train wheels start to chant
But to the dark you whisper *No no no* –

Soul Says

Soul says well let us watch the old night sky
Until the darkness gazes back: your river murmurs as it turns
But will not break our tie

A hundred spiderlings are hanging from this leaf
Their world was silk
Now they await a small warm air to carry them away
They will not cause us any grief

The river slips beneath a net of lights at Auchenflower
I say
Where people cannot sleep for all this sleepy day
When only a river moves

(The smells of mud along the river bank
The new blond towns that court the very worst of heat)

Soul says you catch my drift
Now say some more

I say
Today I heard the beat of parrot wings
And felt a shadow fleeing on my face
My blood ran colder
Than deep and weedy currents down below

Ah stop and watch the spiderlings begin their flight
Soul says
A few may wither in the sac
A few may reach the other shore

The sound you heard above your head was me
Soul says
And for a moment I was almost free:

Now let us go
Now you have felt the darkness gazing back

Those White, Ancient Birds

And so they come, after the darkest month,
As though all guided by the one intelligence:
They play the air,
                but cannot survive on light
Or feed upon the generous heat of day.
They cry their hallilujahs
But wind resists them too, it brings them down,

To settle on a barn roof

Or gather by a pool.

I do not think they know much about longing,
Those white, ancient birds,
                they know just where to go
And fly there, at their appointed time,
Without a weighing up of gains and losses,

But I have no idea where to go,
And wait all morning by a window, the big sky blankly there,
Not knowing what I am waiting for
Yet aching for it just the same.

The River

There is a radiance inside the winter woods
    That calls each soul by name:
Wind in young boughs, trees shaking off thick coats of snow,

The rattle of frozen rain on a barn roof: all these
    Will help you lose your way
And find a silence older than the sky

That makes our being here a murmur only,
    That makes me walk along the river
Beyond where it has flooded itself

While freezing over, past these dead firs,
    The great assembly of cedars,
So that I must say, *I do not know why I am here*,

And move around in those few words
    And feel their many needles
Upon my lips and warm them on my tongue

Though I say nothing, for it is a calm
    Beyond the calm I know
That wants to talk now, after all these years

Of hearing me say *spruce*, *wind*, *cloud* and *face*,
    Not knowing the first thing about them all,
Not knowing the simplest thing,

That every word said well is praise:
    And someone deep inside me wants to say
I am not lost but there are many paths!

While someone else will whisper back,
    So you are on the longest quest of all,
The quest for home, and not appear

Though I have walked along the river now
  These good five miles
While letting wind push me a little way

And letting thoughts grow slow and weak
  Before I feed them words, for what
Is told to me this afternoon

Is simply *river*, with each *I* and *it* dissolved,
  A cold truth but a truth indeed
Held tight on the way back

Past curves and forks, as evening takes hold,
  A strange light all the way
That falls between the words that I would use

When talking of this strangeness or this light
  So that I speak in small, slow breaths
Of evening, cedar, cone and ice

In words that stick to skin –

The Calm

There is a cancer fiddling with its cell of blood
A butcher's knife that's frisking lamb for fat
And then there is the Calm.

All over the world numbers fall off the clocks
But still there is the Calm. There is a sound
Of a clock's hands

And then there is the Calm.

Now there are children playing on a beach
Out on the Marshall Islands
With fallout in their hair, a freak snowfall.
There is no Calm

But then there is the Calm.

All night I feel my old loves rotting in my heart
But morning brings the Calm

Or else the afternoon.

Some days I will say yes, and then odd days
It seems that things say yes to me.
And stranger still, there are those times
When I become a yes

(And they are moments of the Calm).

'True, Like…'

1

Bad saints everywhere.

2

True, like the kiss of a peach.

3

The gods don't live in mirrors.

4

Those sounds of darkness even at noon.

5

True, like the chili's word.

6

A nail to hang your halo on.

7

But still the names of ports drift out to sea.

8

The frank lucidity of pain.

9

I say your name to keep me warm.

10

True, like the brandy's flame.

11

And all the earth between us, holy ground.

September Rain

I'm fine like this, just fine, as evening comes
Like some sad Blues turned on nextdoor
Played low,

No one about, only
Streetlights ready to welcome it
And rain nestling up to them,
                    a rain I hadn't heard till now.

It's Ella Fitzgerald singing 'The Blues are Brewin''
And so the rain comes down, bringing
The evening on its back,

And people quickening along the street,

The day's focus going everywhere.

It's fine, just fine, sitting in my room,
                    down at the back of the house,
My books at rest for the evening;

And prowling down the hall,
A good long smell of frying onion, meaning
I can stay here some more,
                              not putting the light on.

The rain now in a great passion about something,
And Ella getting hard to hear…

Outside, things riding on the surface of the past
And inside,
            the taste of time upon my lips.
It's fine, just fine.

Rain

Late afternoon: rain brushes past the window
And I feel less alone. I know that, soon,
It will all stop; but now it breaks the day
In a procession of days, each shining, whole,

And turns stray minutes into someone's life.
Not mine: in forty years I've never thought
How strange to hold a cup and watch the rain,
The tea gone cold, my finger wandering

Over the rim; and for the first time ever
I feel thick drops of varnish, and take them
As kindnesses, not meant for me but loved
As though they were. The Hassidim will tell

About the life to come, how everything
Will stay the same. That stain upon my chair,
It must remain; my cup cannot be smooth.
This world will be untouched, they nod and say,

But just a little changed. Late afternoon:
I sit here, deep inside this April day,
Half-thanking someone I will never meet,
The rain outside now striking hard and fast.

The Word

There is a word that's set out from my death.
I know it has already left my lips
Although I don't know what on earth I'll say

When that time comes. It circles round the world,
And some dark nights I almost think I hear
The lemon tree out back repeating it.

I know it took the whole of life to say
That single word, and though it might seem weird
I half-imagine it is large enough

For me to live in now, a word so big
I'd never notice it while reading hard
Or find it looking up a dictionary,

That word I say a dozen times a day,
A word that slips my tongue just when you ask,
A word my death will not confide in me.

Beneath the Ode

Just there, beneath the ode, a speck of dust.
You flick it with a little finger. No,
    A spot of ink. But wait:
    Now that you look up close,
It is a word. Quick, magnify the thing!

Good Lord, there are two words, no, three or more,
All blowing up like helium balloons.
    And so your hand transcribes,
    And so the glass falls down:
The words all shrivel to a dot again

As though graffitied on a baby's eye.
But who? An angel pausing from the dance?
    You take another book
    And there it is, that spot.
So was it always there but never seen,

Or has it come on just this summer day
Along with letters, clouds, a line of ants?
    It is a strange strange world,
    This one in which we live.
Whom do you call, the cops or cardinals?

Do state police answer the phone these days?
Is there a prefix for the Vatican?
    The questions multiply
    While in each book you own
Each poem edges closer to that dot.

Soul Says

Young sparrows in the ivy says the ear
Young sparrows there!
But eye is brooding on those thunderclouds up high
Now blowing in from south, and mind

Is combing through old words at home
Back there

All wrong, soul says,
All wrong each way from lip to lees:

A stone luxuriates in stone inside its lair
As you walk past,
Not looking at your orange trees in bloom
Or listening for corn caressed by harvest breeze

And all our day the – the impossible
Is sizing up the possible, just trying it this way and that
And then engaging, fast

Come children, now –
You ear and eye and mind, you others too –
I say,
Come and be gathered in a word

That feels its way through forking ivy veins
In our back yard,
That feels the blank beyond what words can bear

(Poor word, soul says,
That lets the sunlight through)

And all our day the – the impossible
Is sizing up the possible, just trying it this way and that
And then engaging, hard

One day, soul says,

One day, I say,

One day
The eye and mind will listen, and abide

Wimmera Songs

Late in the night up north, in that hard land past Nhill,
When cold comes through your boots
And when the last stars wave 'Farewell, farewell'

And mallee fowl stir on their mound

And tracks no one has used for many years
Begin to feel around
For guinea flowers, stones, and roots,

You see a radiance
Before the sun begins to climb a wide gray sky
And spill across the wilderness;

And then the soul rejoices, remembering that light
Over burnt grass

That utters nothing you can say

But gives you life to act it out.

*

Up in the Little Desert there are yellow gums
And giant redgums
That brood at campsites of the Tatyara and Tallagiera;

Whipsticks
And snakes that scribble on sand,

Fierce scarlet bottlebrush
And tiny orchids flicking out their tongues.

*

Out in the Big Desert
You learn just how to peel your words
And need to drink their juice:

One day I will live there,
Inside the sun, and make my peace with time,
And make a friend of silence;

Yet in good years
Poets forget the desert's lenten homilies,
Its sand dunes shaped like tears,

And move down south
Where warm swamps all wear Fairies' Aprons
And yellow marsh flowers float upon the water.

*

In January at Murrayville
Only the river moves;
Sky quivers with its weight of sun:
Noon heat cracks wattle seeds.

But in the Grampians, at dusk,
Before young rats come out,
You walk with clouds caught in your hair
Past ghosts that cling to rocks.

*

O Desert,
One vision of wildflowers in five years
Is not enough.

*

In the Big Desert there is a silence that welcomes you
But if you stay
You find the other silence that fits your head inside a vice.

*

There is an excellence
In going up to Minyip for a month in summer
And gazing at a field of sunflowers one afternoon
While reading the *Parmenides*:

The stranger we call Being
Makes patterns in wheatfields before dawn,
And iron tanks, set deep in earth,
Say the few, simple things that must be heard.

*

And yet the radiance
Slips back into the other world, leaving a frail light
Around young redgums by the river.

Stretch out upon this yellow grass
And listen to a blue wren
And learn its lesson:

Think like a cloud

Go where clouds go.

Nights

1

Somehow I had to learn to sleep alone.
Each night the lessons droned on hour on hour,
And someone – was it you? – kept phoning me
Then hanging up, once I put out the light.

Like stupid kids, my mind fought with my heart,
Made up, then of a sudden went for blood.
Those fuckers smashed up everything in sight
And where was I to stop them, where were you?

2

All summer long you vanished bit by bit.
I watched you slowly turn into yourself:
Your study was a bedroom, then a fort.
You went from 'I've a cold' to 'I'm confused',

And then, quite suddenly, you left for good.
For weeks I festered with an angry guilt,
And then for months I blazed with hidden light,
And then, one day, a year had passed me by.

Fed up with sleeping with a crazy man,
The cat moved from the bottom of our bed
And claimed the space you left. 'Good girl,' I said,
Then slept, warm darkness purring in my ear.

3

The police helicopter hangs overhead.
Ah, how you hated it: night after night
They'd circle round our block and maybe cast
A searchlight down the lane. 'Those fucking cops',

'They must be landing on our fucking roof,'
You cried one night. It *was* well after two
And, truth be told, we had just gone to bed.
The law came nosing through our half-closed blinds

And framed us, actors in a porno film.
'More light! more light!' I mumbled half asleep,
But you were half-way down the hall by then,
In search of condoms, justice, or a drink.

4

Nights, you would turn to me in bed: no face,
A voice only, barely a voice, a breath.
It was as though the darkness whispered, 'Love,
'Touch me, take all this worry from my head,'

And I would place my hands over your brow
And tell you they were probing deep inside,
Then slowly draw out every trouble there.
I had to teach you how to fall asleep.

You left in winter, and it's winter now.
It takes all day to fill the house with light.
On days like this we'd go on long, long walks
Around the parks, stop in a warm café

Half-fogged with coffee and the latest talk,
Come home, make love, and then make love again.
The house remembers everything we did:
I hear you walking barefoot on cold tiles.

And so the light goes out in certain words,
Home, *children*, *morning*, *wine*, and even *you*.
I've frisked the house for anything you've left
And pushed my furniture this way, then that –

You'd hardly recognise the place, or me.
I threw away my photographs of you,
But other images soon took their place:
You in the kitchen, too impatient for lunch,

A lick of honey hanging from your chin;
Those summer nights the year we fell in love:
'My darling,' you would say, 'drink from my mouth,'
Your long eyelashes brushing past my lips.

5

I spend too many hours just thinking of you.
A book before me, or a glass of wine –
It hardly matters. I don't take much in.
I've picked my life down to the very bone.

There's no way that I'll ever win you back:
I'd just as easily get chairs to dance.
And yet these nights with nothing on my mind
Or stirring in my heart, I think of you.

After Hölderlin

High summer grass bends to the brimming lake:
Pears thick with juice
Hang down with the wild roses.
                              Ah, necking swans,

You're drunk,
But keep on drinking from each other's eyes,
Then dunk your heads
Into the lustral water.

Tell me, where will I find flowers
Sunshine and shade
When winter comes this way?

Nothing but walls
With their backs turned, and wind
Rattles the weathercock.

Her Kiss

He knew that it was many years ago
　　When he first loved her, when he met
Her in a restaurant with him, and that
The blurry feeling when he saw her smile
　　At work or in a supermarket queue

Meant he had been a tangent to his life.
　　He knew all that; but only when,
One day, he heard himself pronounce her name
To someone passing in the corridor,
　　And was surprised by tenderness,

He understood that it was far too late,
　　That old mistakes will multiply
Inside the heart, or cancel themselves out.
But which was it? Well, she was married now
　　And surely never thought of him

Like that, then he remembered how she looked
　　When someone hugged him in the bar,
How e-mail from her ending 'With regards'
Had changed to 'Yours'. He lived inside her kiss
　　Two weeks before the moment came

And three days after. When she turned to him,
　　And he could see the downy hairs
Above her lips, his hands reached round her back,
And all her fascination was condensed
　　Into a kiss that neither felt

Till later in their separated homes:
　　When putting children down to sleep,
When lying with the darkness all around.
He touched again the ridges of her spine,
　　She knew the hungers of his mouth.

170

Nineteen Songs

Today I think that love
Is simply watching her
Peeling a mandarin
(As though an entire life
Could turn on fingertips)

I have not spared my eyes
Since I became a man
And yet I little thought
That I would feel desire
For fingers sprayed with juice

Today I looked ahead
And sitting opposite
Saw her select some fruit
And quickly pierce its skin
With a fine fingernail

How little it will seem
Enclosed in memory,
Sharing that mandarin
(But two entire lives
Turned on her fingertips)

*

Two yellow tulips in a bottle
That held red wine last night;

Small islands of fermenting green
Played samba in your sleep,

I woke up to admire the way
Your blouse fell on my clock:

I want to love you all the day
With the lightness of blossom,

I want to love you all the night
With the density of hammers

*

Just sometimes when she speaks
Across the table
Content with claret, ham and cheese
Her voice goes deep
And at that moment (and no other)
She could take my soul

And sometimes when she tears
A hunk of bread
And soaks it in the olive oil
She does not speak
And at that moment (and no other)
She could take my soul

*

I only want to lay my head upon your lap
And let my hands meet round your waist
I only want to rest and hear you talk awhile
And breathe the perfume of your words

Men simply look at you and fall in love again:
I only want the world to turn
A little faster now so they fall off the globe
And a great turtle eats them up

I only want to live forever in your kiss
And let my hands slip down your thighs
I only want your eyes and breasts to say my name
And your light hand undo my belt

*

172

I like to drench my face
In your thick hair, and lick
Where neck and shoulder meet.
There is a fine gray hair
I love, near your left lobe:
God's captured by a hair!
Exclaimed my patron saint
(My patron poet too)
And I know how He feels

I like to laze an hour
Just gazing in your eyes
And see my future there.
There is a small brown spot
I love, beside a lash:
An eye has wounded me!
Exclaimed my patron saint
(My patron poet too)
And I know how he feels

*

Simply to touch her hand
And know the undertow
Of feelings without names
That pulls my mouth to hers,

To listen for the laugh
That falls between her words
And live there all the week,
A lazy animal,

To run my fingertips
So slowly down her thigh
And feel the honey thicken
Inside my newfound flesh,

To ease her heavy hair
Away from ear and shoulder
The better to kiss her neck
And hear her saying *Yes,*

So that the bees will dance
So that the lion feeds
So that the truth is told
So that the ocean lives

*

When evening stills the birds
I listen to the trees
And think of her at home:

> *Whenever you fall in love*
> *It is for the first time*

At night there are few words
And I trust only those
That taste still of her lips:

> *Whenever you fall in love*
> *It is for the first time*

My pillow stole one hair;
I feel the warmth she left
But think of her with him:

> *Whenever you fall in love*
> *It is for the first time*

*

My gladness is to fall asleep with you
In your old nightgown with a hole in it

(Sometimes we go to bed with a fine wine
Sometimes there's lamplight and our simple talk)

My pleasure is to run a finger down
Your spine and pray a little on each ridge

(Sometimes we turn our bedside lamp way down
Sometimes there's moonlight, sometimes only eyes)

My joy is just to kiss you where I can
And make your lips go soft, your nipples hard

(I wake up with a gray hair on my cheek
Or a dark curly one upon my tongue)

*

I think that hardly anyone
Has ever fallen very far:
There are so many safety nets
There are so many nooses tied

For when you truly fall in love
Each glass of wine is tasted twice:
Because each sip is for her too
Because each sip means twice as much

I think that hardly anyone
Has ever fallen very far:
So many men walk round and round
So many men just will not jump

For when you truly fall in love
The sun comes closer by a mile:
It is enough to make you sweat
It is enough to make you strip

*

On Monday we made love for the first time
And then, on Tuesday morning, once you left,

I polished the hall mirror, working in
The cream in long, slow strokes for half an hour,

Then rubbing hard until I saw myself
For the first time, though when I looked up close

I realised that you were gazing back
And calling me while saying your own name:

And so the mirror clouded with my breath
And so I took to polishing again

On Tuesday afternoon, when you were out,
Before we made wild love all Wednesday night

*

Sometimes you wake me up
When you are days away
In Tübingen or Bath
By entering my dream
With very little on:
Perhaps that new white bra
And those silk panties that
Ride up a little way,
Or maybe just a smile

Well, I am waiting here
In our big double bed
With nothing much to do
Except read Schelling twice:
So why not fly straight home
Just as you are today
From Tübingen or Bath
With cardigan and coat
And I'll wear just a smile

*

Rain falls on Carlton North
As evening blows in:
It is the wildest rain
That ever graced my roof,

And when I look outside
It rushes through a light
As though to say 'It's late,
And soon you must decide,'

I lean upon a pane
And almost see her face
Behind the streaming glass
Though truly it is mine,

And she unlocks a door
Half-way across the town:
Perhaps wind lifts her gown
With wicked little claw;

Perhaps she thinks it kind,
Perhaps it reaches high
Along each pretty thigh,
Perhaps... ah, lucky wind

*

Away from home, friends fill my plate
With berries dazed with armagnac
But in my bed I'm hungry still

And there all night I fill my mouth
With your sweet name

I like to bite into firm plums
And let a finger stroke the fuzz
That lightly covers a white peach

Yet still I love to roll my tongue
Around your name

Away from you, I love to touch
The skin of a young tangerine
Or weigh a ripe pear in my palm

But nothing feeds me half so well
As your sweet name

*

Let others be good boys and go to work
I want to stay in bed with you all day

What's wrong with coffee, very strong and black,
Then squandering the whole damn day at lunch?

Let others teach and fill in all the forms
While we dip sugar cubes into champagne

And when we wander through the cemetery
Even the oldest graves will stir a bit

Tonight I want your tongue inside my mouth
My semen hot and wild inside your cunt

*

Just sometimes when you are away
One of my hands will touch my cheek
So lightly, like your hand at night,
And then I am in bed with you

And sometimes when you are right here
One of my hands will stroke your cheek:
It reaches slowly down your spine
And soon I am in bed with you

*

I want to enter you
Like a young lion that strides
Into the Serengeti
While locusts chant nightfall.
He flicks off tsetse flies,
Stalks in savannah grass
Then pounces – muscles hard,
And wild mane flying high –
Upon an antelope

When I lie beside you
On a dry summer night
Perhaps I am a lion,
But all the rest is false:
You are not Africa,
You are all sleepy, warm,
The one who feeds my heart,
And – now I feel down there –
All of a sudden, wet

*

I think that truth is always clothed in love,
So when I say 'I feel the infinite'

And you are breathing slowly in my arms
No syllable is stretched beyond its bound,

So when my fingers roam around your thigh
And I can bring myself to speak, only

The simple truth is murmured: 'You are all',
So when I enter you, and your warm mouth

Absorbs me in a night without a day
And a wild rhythm builds without a word

The truth is told just then, by eyes that close,
By lips and fingertips, by tongue and cock

*

Sometimes when I reach out to touch your arm
One of the bad angels has stretched
Both time and space, and you
Are somewhere in Germany last century

And sometimes when I move to hold your hand
There is no space or time at all:
For I am there already,
Your fingertips are lightly playing mine

And always when I lean to kiss your eyes
One of the good angels has told
A fib for me, and I
Am in your eyes already: shining, whole

*

I walk beside a stream
And feel the sunlight age
Upon my arms and face:
Only your touch gives life

I think of how you came
So suddenly to me:
As though God simply wiped
Horizons from the earth

Sweet love, come take my hand:
It is the strangest day
The first of all the world
Because of your caress

The shortest day will come
But God will look at us
And know himself at last:
And you will kiss his lips

'How Hast Thou Counselled Him...'

You say that nights like this must come from far away,
Arising from 'the empty place'
Where He 'hangeth the earth upon nothing'.

A warm night – scented with mangoes and white wine –
But there is something lost.

You point outside, and I can see a last
Proud blue give way

That silences the very sparrows in my roof.

A final, delicate weight
Has tipped the great scales all at once

And it is night for ever

But warm
         as though night were always here
Inside me,
         like my breathing in the small hours
Once sleep has untied this knot and that
And taken me so far.

Rare nights like this must venture here from far away
And deep inside...

See: the sky is slowly drained, and then the night
Descends into the darkness of the heart

And glides for hours.

The Bird Is Close

Half-dreaming and naked, I am laying dresses over my left arm
    While night blows through our bedroom window:
Here are the easy florals of summer

    And here a velvet gown whose crimson folds I love…
How strange a thing in the wee hours
    When the only sound is a flutter of a bird's wings

    And that heard just the once.

A whisper of feathers in a wardrobe near an open window
    And I am handling silk and tulle
For mother,

    And it is 1963, so nothing is ever lost
I tell myself, except

    It is 1989 and I am laying out her clothes
After the funeral and wondering what to do with them.
    Years later, a sound, half-heard, of wings at night,

Is making me go further in the dark
    While my wife sits on our bed in a little lamplight
Feeding our new daughter

    Who startles when I bring down a box.

And I am shivering now in the warm summer night
    For I know the bird is close
With a wing broken perhaps and eyes as wild as mine,

    But there's a final box, with faded maps,
A notebook brimming with sweet days.

                              Inside the wardrobe now,
Crouched down
        And sweating, as if covered in black felt,
I have crossed a line I did not know was there:

              I cannot see my hands
But they are holding the bird, tightly and tenderly,

        Before I touch the bird.

'L'Intelligence avec l'ange'

(for Robert Adamson)

I get up earlier these days, and leave
The house in darkness, scooping up my child
With mother's milk still clinging to her chin,
So that my wife can sleep. It is just light

In Princes Park, and Sarah is asleep
Just like her mother, now a mile away.
Before I left I let my fingers stray
Around my books, not turning on the light:

Now, sitting on a bench, I see the dark
Has given me *Feuillets d'Hypnos*. Yes,
A fine edition with pages roughly cut.
No one around: my mouth curves round those notes

Char scribbled on the run, inflamed by war,
And I translate one for my sleeping child –
'The fruit is blind. It is the tree that sees' –
Because she likes to look up at the leaves,

Then read again the one I know by heart,
About an angel living deep inside
That speaks the highest silence that there is.
I stumbled through a moment left ajar

And stayed two hours. Now Sarah rubs her eyes,
I drink some icy water from a tap,
And walk back home beside the Cemetery.
Your new poems flew here while I was out:

Both speak 'a meaning that we cannot count'.
I read them out aloud while Sarah feeds
And help myself to coffee, warm white rolls
And the dark honey that teaches us to sing.

V

1999-2000

The Little Air

1

First thing on a winter morning there was ice
Inside the window: I'd scrape it with my nails.
The pipes outside were sometimes frozen stiff
And kids would double dare each other hard

To see whose fingerprints of flesh would stick,
But when we got to school there would be knives
Of ice that hung from classroom windowsills,
And we would throw them at each other's eyes

While running mad: you'd breathe the little air
That felt just like those needles in your cheeks
And hope the bell for class would go off now,
Though when it did we were all in for it.

2

When I was ten, in Mr F.'s bad class,
There was a girl with glasses and thin legs
Called Millie Steele. She'd gather us around
And tell us stories made up as she spoke

About a Green Line Bus that went too far,
About a girl who lived beneath a pond...
I still remember how her lips would move.
One dress-up day she came as an old witch

And everyone could see the truth in that
And gave her hell. Her mum was pretty, though,
'All done up like a Christmas dinner, eh?',
My mother said one night when dad got home

From drinking in a pub down Barking way,
'And deep into her Pims with Mr Wrong?'
But next day Millie spun a lovely tale
How mum's mascara bled into her face.

3

'Pamela Baker?' Mr F. would ask
Each chilly day at morning roll, and smile,
And I would too, but very secretly,
Her long brown hair cast back onto my desk...

4

A retired major, Mr F. could paint
And did so every day before the class,
Just conning, stroke by stroke, a Constable.
It took a year for him to get one right.

I'd write a story, do his weekly quiz,
And watch him out the front with brush in hand.
Three decades on, I saw my year, for him,
Was making 'Hadleigh Castle' almost his.

At break we kicked a sodden football round
And, if the smog was bad that winter's day,
Played hide-and-seek by standing very still
In thick gray air, just waiting to be found.

One day I hid behind the big uns' rooms
When F. was on his tour around the yard.
(He marched, erect, with a long, yellow cane
That beat against his leg at morning hymns.)

He spied me with his little eye, his fist
Came through the blur and pulled me back in bounds.
I saw his stick; he tried to grab my hand;
He got the fingertips, then struck my wrist.

5

Our living-room had dresses hanging limp
With pins around the hem and darts tacked in,
And every night when dad was off at work
Some were alive with girls from Romford, Bow,

Or Becontree: they sat on our old couch
In panties and a bra and talked for hours
About the local clubs and groups and boys
While I was Popeye. Once, two tizzy blondes

Sat either side and tried to make me blush;
They stroked my legs, and whispered silly things
I mostly missed because they giggled so.
One taught me how to kiss when mum slipped out,

The other said I really was a one.
Mum thought I was a mummy's boy: I was,
Although she learned to pluck me from the girls
And hide the needles for my catapult.

6

The tension in mum's Singer was all wrong;
It filled the room. She ripped out, row by row.
And when I took another Granny Smith,
Spat out, 'That fruit don't grow on trees, you know!'

7

Sweet Lord, there was an Irish girl called Clare
Who lived nextdoor but one to Nanna's house.
We never played but once, because her hair
Was made of fire, her body mad with lice.

Her father had gone off one moonless night,
My Grandad said. We'd hear her mother cry
All bloody afternoon when she was tight
And we were slow with Nanna's kidney pie

And cups of tea. One Sunday, on the rack,
My Grandad slung the front door open loud
And barked out, 'Shuttup, that won't bring 'im back!'
His army voice had half the neighbours cowed.

'Old mother's ruin, needle 'n' pin,' Nan said,
And digged my mother firmly in the ribs.
But I saw Clare outside, sweet Lord, her head
On fire, her dress all torn. 'Lips thick with fibs,'

My mother snipped, but Clare was looking hard
Into our backyard window – a white face
That knew a week or two of bread and lard –
Right through the glass, right through the plastic lace.

8

My future was a khaki envelope
And when it came, without the slightest fuss,
I knew just what it was: 'Eleven plus'
Had slept with me, although I had no hope

Of ending somewhere in the grammar zone,
Or so old Benfield told my folks one night
While cycling home, and he was almost right.
I was a mile beneath my skin and bone,

A light about an inch from any lens
And never getting closer. I was 'slow'
I heard my mother say with me in tow
Down Heathrow shops. I doodled in the men's

While she was telling all the smelly town,
And wrote *KH* in half a dozen ways
Then listened to my mother in a daze
Though never met her softly studied frown,

For she was right. I didn't trust their world.
And when the letter came that autumn day
I slyly looked to see what it would say
And found I didn't understand a word.

9

But birds I understood all right, oh yes,
I knew each robin's nest in Parsloe's Park
And knew my way there even in the dark.
I'd climb a tree and feel those warm small eggs,

Then slither down, and slowly walk around
Although my heart was beating something bad.
(One winter's night, round there, I saw my dad
High on his bike, off late from the day shift.)

It was a night like that, while sloping home,
A bloke in drainpipes stopped me at those bins
Next to our pub. I saw him there, all grins,
And walked on. But he seemed to know our mum,

And talked about the girls who came around,
And if I knew the name of that thin one
With the suede coat and hair all up in bun.
He'd like to leave his mark on that there girl,

He said, he'd like to do a lot of things
(And as he spoke I smelled a game of darts),
Oh yes, and then unzipped his hairy parts,
And held them, looking hard at me, and hard.

10

On winter days the milk had always been
Before I woke: four bottles had a sweat
Around our old gas fire or talked of debt
Beside the scuttle, taking coal for kin.

Our mum was at her Singer by half eight.
'*Needle 'n' pin,*' she sang, '*needle 'n' pin.*'
Her girls were never rude and often thin.
(Their boys would lean for hours beside our gate.)

The coal man came on Wednesday afternoon
When it was dark. He cracked a crooked grin
And heaved a bag of black into our bin.
Dad said his duchess scarpered off one June.

On Friday nights it was the Paraffin.
Mum always sent me out, in snow or slush.
His fingers shook; he fell; his face was mush.
('*Needle 'n' pin,*' she snapped, '*needle 'n' pin.*')

The Hall

1

All summer long, the smell of gums in heat:

And every night I've thought of that old hall
On Tavistock, left on a scrap of land
Near Oxley Station:
                                those Inala boys
Gave a new coloured kid what for, near there,
While he was waiting for the late train home.

That was in January '69,
And when, come light, they found him in long grass
Around the back, 'he was set neat and still',
The local paper said.
                                There were tyre marks,
And someone found a knuckleduster there.

It happened – broke out in a time and place.

A narrow building, made of great long planks
All painted pink: it stood on short, thick stumps,
CWA in ragged loops of white.

Some days that year, as summer dragged along,
I'd half-imagine other trains would come
With country women, yards of rusty white
All flapping madly round their ample calves,

Descending on the hall from Quilpe, Miles,
Their bags stacked up beside a sugargum.

Some days, I'd wander down the hill from school
With a warm girl just out from Surinam,
And take her round the back, in a wild patch

Of shade, and we'd sit there a quarter hour,
And I would run a finger up her leg
Until I touched her knee, while talking low

Of this and that,
                    right up from her white sock
So very slowly till I reached her knee,
And sometimes higher if her train was late...

2

The Missionary Baptist Church met there
On Sundays for some seven years or so:
Lost locals, mostly, and those homely folk

Straight out from Little Rock in Arkansas
Who sang us songs like 'Yield to Jesus Christ'
(The preacher holding up a 'GIVE WAY' sign)

And bluesy southern hymns that squeezed the heart
On humid nights, after a thunderstorm.
There was a business man of forty-odd,

Red in the face, and running fast to fat,
Who quietly shook my hand while coming in
And let thick tears pour slowly down his cheeks

When the conversion hymn, 'Just as I am',
Was struck up by the preacher's pretty girl
(A chord a finger wrong in the first verse).

But a long sermon was the hot event:
'Woe unto thee that scattereth abroad!'
The preacher cried one night, then flailed and wailed

And lost his way, and told that sinners spend
Eternity with fingers scratching boards.
I always thought the big red man would break

And stumble up the front, without one plea,
And say, 'I'm saved! Praise thee, Lord Jesus Christ!'
We'd all done that; we'd all been flicked by flame;

Even that woman with a touch of lace
Who lived alone on Cliveden Avenue,
Who'd drenched the preacher's vast white shirt one night,

193

Then turned to us, before the girl could stop,
And screeched, 'I've sinned against the Holy Ghost!'
She walked, less shaken than we were, straight back,

And placed her Bible firmly on her lap.
The preacher gave a crowd a lift, that night,
Accelerating past the Greek café

(Inala boys with flick-knives, cadging chips...)
And I sat near a girl who used lipstick,
And when we stopped outside that woman's house

That preacher went right in, and turned on lights,
And checked her cupboard slowly, dress by dress:
The two of us alone in his back seat,

Our fingers meeting somewhere near her leg;
The V8 grumbling underneath us both,
The air on fire, lights clicking off and on.

194

Madonna

1

Some rich black hair hangs idly over her left breast
And as her head lolls back
A wild old blues begins to slip
                              between the little bones inside her neck
And work its slow way down o down her spine
And when she turns

Onto her side, beside the open window,
                              her longest tress plays lightly on the small
Of her long back.

Her eyes are softly closed
                              (the music may be wine,
My sweet words singing in their nest of breath,
A sobbing that she keeps deep down inside
                              where I can never go).

Dear Lord, these are the lips
                              that taste of moonlight, salt and oil

And just behind them
                              a tongue that feels around

In the zucchini flower

2

'Death and desire': I saw the exhibition years ago,
In Brisbane,
                  deep in January's honey heat:

I walked into the gallery
With a young girl I loved, and said I loved worlds more,

And looked at things I thought I knew
Like summer nights and kissing pretty girls

Or when the mind goes limp
                    and lets death rise
And flood your house with kennel bones and clay.

I looked at that 'Self-Portrait' with the long skeletal arm
And thought about my soul
While she was looking somewhere else,

Then sat before 'Madonna'
And knew the mouth and lids I longed to kiss

But knew no woman like her, not at all,
No woman given to the dark,

And then I felt an arm around my shoulders
And so we kissed

And then walked out

And let the heat rise up and carry us away

    3
There was a girl I loved when I was seventeen
And every summer night that year
                    I'd shower, put on icy jeans,
Walk Oxley Station Road, then turn
Down Blunder, and

Soon spend an æon cruising California:

A water glass and flask beside a bedroom window,
Mosquito coils all smouldering in hot, dark rooms.

Perhaps I'd spy her once a week
When she was at her desk, in lamplight, doing History,
Or telling diary about him,

The school beach boy
With yellow hair who played guitar in clubs;

(And then one night she was out front
Just hosing pink geraniums,

Barefoot, in a short cotton dress.

And I remember something rising in her eyes
That I could almost taste

And how she cast her long dark hair way back:
Something about her voice
                              when talking of that new LP
Or how she spent the whole day down the coast
Where little fish flicked right between her legs.

The sound of people talking low nearby, after a beer or two,
The smell of cigarettes on a long, humid summer night,

Her brown feet in the thick crab grass)

    4

                              'In the beginning was sex,'
A friend of Munch's declared in print, with him in mind,
Over a century ago, in 1893,
                    two years before 'Madonna', hanging on my wall,
Had been conceived.

Some see that bold half-truth
In sperm that fly around the frame, while other folk
Point to the embryo
                    kept by itself down left

Where there's no edge,
                              where darkness is let out
Or in, depending how you understand its gaze.

And other men, like me, don't point at all
But simply say
                    it is the way her mouth relaxes there,
The way a shadow lives inside her curves,

                    the way her eyes, even half-closed,
Halve any room she's in:

197

So when you walk
                into that loudly crowded ball
Of cream and gold and filligree,
And when your fingertips must leave the door
And your gaze settles down,

You're at her side,

No matter where you are
                    no matter who you are
No matter who she is

   5

A year after I saw that retrospective, just by chance,
With her,

The one I thought I'd marry before long,
The one I'd taken home that summer,

The one of whom my mother said, 'She's nice'
While lighting up a cigarette

And looking out the window
That showed a jacaranda tree that made the breeze so sweet,

My mother was quite firmly put to bed
With a bad cancer.

When I flew home to see her
It turned out she was sleeping on the couch, where it was cool,

And so I slept with father
In their big double bed: we whispered late into the night

Until she'd scream
And he'd get up and go to her. So no one got much sleep,

Though sometimes I would slip
Into the sewing room where we were billeted the year before

With a black Singer for straight stitching,
Electric scissors, pinned-up wedding dresses hanging from a wall,

And stretch out on the camp bed that we used
And try to cancel myself out.

The first night we were there, in bed, just talking in the lamplight,
About cicadas, sweat,

And spending all tomorrow idling on a riverboat,
My mother pushed the door ajar,

Looked hard
And said, 'I wouldn't get up to anything on that old canvas thing'

6

When I was twenty-two I came back home
To spend a summer doing nothing much:

So I read Schelling, badly, once or twice
While lying on my bed
Where years before I had read Shelley well,

And then, one afternoon,
I stomped, barefoot, down to the shops to hang around

And met her walking out the bakery:
One of the girls I'd known at school, had kissed one night

At some dark party where I'd gone
With cheap wine and another girl
                              who spoke a smoky French
And studied art at some weird place in town.

Her favourite painter of all time
Was a Norwegian, Edvard Munch,

Who said things like 'I was born dying',
And made his pictures up by scraping them away:

She drank neat gin and ice, then passed out very cold
Before the dancing and the smoking and the rest...

*

'Feel it, it's warm,' she said,
And so it was, and while we talked I licked flour off my hand
Then wrote her number there:

For three long days the world looked back at me
With her green eyes,
                          then three days later on I drove us both
To a motel way down the Ipswich Road

And wrote 'Mr and Mrs Bakerman'
                          in my old Queensland hand
Then somehow walked into a room
That might have been gift-wrapped in cellophane.

What I remember best
Is standing just inside the door and holding her, my head deep in
                          her hair,
No word between us: gently swaying back and forth
Inside a truth in bud,
                          my fingers joining at the small of her long back,
The coolness of her lips upon my neck:

The two of us just rocking in each other's arms,
O back and forth there, back and forth

Nights

Midnight, she's up and walking out the back
In bare feet, looking at a winter moon,
With flat chinotto in a coffee mug.
(I'm half-asleep and slowly stretching out
Down the hypoteneuse of our old bed.)

It's three o'clock: she's reading magazines
And eating stale *risotto con funghi*
Straight from the fridge with that fierce chili sauce.
(I'm pulling down a pillow to hold tight
That smells a little of her new perfume.)

At five she's dragged the blankets over her
And left a radio just barely on
And, yes, forgotten to turn off a light.
(I wake up saying I'll do anything
And find the cat is staring in my eyes.)

By six the sun is playing with our blind
And children are all back inside their beds;
Somehow the bedroom smells of wine and rice.
(Still half-asleep, my hand goes home to her.
She wakes up saying she'll do anything.)

Amo Te Solo

Sometimes a life goes wrong
Without an evil deed:
So here I am in Berne
Awake in the white hours
Waiting for time to pass
Until I can call home

    For when I am away
    Each hour leaves its bruise

Late home, my cab drives down
Small streets whose names I love;
The evening is ripe
With sparrows and a breeze;
An outside light shines round
And tightly holds the house

    There is no life on earth
    I would not spend with you

*

Love is a standing to attention. Yes,
No man can argue long against a truth
That smashes hard into his deepest life

It's spring: the maple tree speaks of her lips,
The curve around her bottom that I love.
But no one sane will ever quote a tree,

So I must tell her how this little world
Is bigger now only because of her,
And how this massive universe makes sense

Only because of her (it does, it does),
And how this ordinary room is love
And truth because she walks through it all day

*

It is a dark green ivy afternoon
In Princes Hill as rain falls through vast trees
Into the little garden where we live
    On summer days.

It's late December and the clocks have stopped
While people watch their windows come alive
And old tin roofs out back get hopping mad
    And gutters booze.

Last week we burned our flesh, but now we baste
While smoky jazz just cruises down the lane
And makes out with our cat beneath a car
    While we're in bed,

The sheets all trampled underneath our feet,
Those lyrics touching us as night comes on:
Something about a day spent drinking wine
    And getting laid

Prayer

O come, in any way you want,
In morning sunlight fooling in the leaves
Or in thick bouts of rain that soak my head

Because of what the darkness said

Or come, though far too slowly for my eye to see,
Like a dark hair that fades to gray

Come with the wind that wraps my house

Or winter light that slants upon a page

Because the beast is stirring in its cage

Or come in raw and ragged smells
Of gumleaves dangling down at noon
Or in the undertow of love
When she's away

Because a night creeps through the day

Come as you used to, years ago,
When I first fell for you

In the deep calm of an autumn morning
Beginning with the cooing of a dove

Because of love, the lightest love

Or if that's not your way these days
Because of me, because
Of something dead in me,
Come like a jagged knife into my gut

Because your touch will surely cut

Come any way you want

But come

BLOODAXE BOOKS

FLEUR ADCOCK
JOHN AGARD
ANNA AKHMATOVA
GILLIAN ALLNUTT
MONIZA ALVI
YVES BONNEFOY
JEAN 'BINTA' BREEZE
BASIL BUNTING
AIMÉ CÉSAIRE
RENÉ CHAR
INGER CHRISTENSEN
STEWART CONN
DAVID CONSTANTINE
IMTIAZ DHARKER
PETER DIDSBURY
STEPHEN DOBYNS
MAURA DOOLEY
HELEN DUNMORE
JACQUES DUPIN
G.F. DUTTON
MENNA ELFYN
PAUL ÉLUARD
HANS MAGNUS ENZENSBERGER
ROY FISHER
CAROLYN FORCHÉ
TUA FORSSTRÖM
TESS GALLAGHER
PHILIP GROSS
GUILLEVIC
JOSEF HANZLÍK
TONY HARRISON
MIGUEL HERNÁNDEZ
KEVIN HART
W.N. HERBERT
RITA ANN HIGGINS
SELIMA HILL
ELLEN HINSEY
FRIEDRICH HÖLDERLIN
MIROSLAV HOLUB
FRANCES HOROVITZ
IOANA IERONIM
PHILIPPE JACCOTTET
KATHLEEN JAMIE
JENNY JOSEPH

ATTILA JÓZSEF
KAPKA KASSABOVA
JACKIE KAY
BRENDAN KENNELLY
GALWAY KINNELL
JOHN KINSELLA
DENISE LEVERTOV
GWYNETH LEWIS
FEDERICO GARCÍA LORCA
OSIP MANDELSTAM
JACK MAPANJE
HENRI MICHAUX
ADRIAN MITCHELL
JULIE O'CALLAGHAN
MICHEAL O'SIADHAIL
GYÖRGY PETRI
J.H. PRYNNE
PETER READING
EVGENY REIN
PIERRE REVERDY
CAROL RUMENS
SAPPHO
GJERTRUD SCHNACKENBERG
ELENA SHVARTS
KEN SMITH
EDITH SÖDERGRAN
PIOTR SOMMER
MARIN SORESCU
ESTA SPALDING
PAULINE STAINER
SALAH STÉTIÉ
ANNE STEVENSON
GEORGE SZIRTES
RABINDRANATH TAGORE
PIA TAFDRUP
R.S. THOMAS
TOMAS TRANSTRÖMER
MARINA TSVETAYEVA
CHASE TWICHELL
LILIANA URSU
PAUL VALÉRY
C.K. WILLIAMS
JAMES WRIGHT
YANG LIAN

Bloodaxe Books has a world-renowned international list of writers.
For a complete catalogue listing hundreds of poetry titles, please write to:
Bloodaxe Books Ltd, Highgreen, Tarset, Northumberland NE48 1RP
or visit our website: **www.bloodaxebooks.com**